Advance Praise for
A Young Innovator's Guide to STEM

"Gitanjali Rao is an inspiring innovator and motivational speaker about her experiences as America's Top Young Scientist. In her book, she provides an infrastructure to help students, teachers, and parents solve real-world problems in a way that can lead to real change. As a former educator, district leader, and STEM thought leader, I highly recommend this book to anyone interested in becoming an innovator to make the world a better place."

—DR. CINDY MOSS, VP, Global STEM, Discovery Education

"Gitanjali has done a remarkable job breaking down the process of innovation—all the way from developing the curiosity and mindset of an innovator, to competing in global competitions. It is a very fun, fast read, with plenty of rich strategies and tips that are clearly drawing on her experience as a young innovator. She doesn't shy away from sharing her hesitations at each step—brainstorming can feel unproductive, research can feel intimidating, teamwork can be slow—but for every roadblock, she provides strategies for overcoming the mindset and practical tips for moving past the roadblocks. Well done, Gitanjali! I hope each and every kid in the world reads this book and realizes that nothing stops them from innovating and making the world better. What an awesome message!"

—TARA CHKLOVSKI, Founder and CEO, Technovation

"Gitanjali's thoughtful insights and step-by-step guidance provide practical lessons for creative thinkers and problem solvers to build crucial real-world skills for personal growth and impactful innovation. A role model herself, Gitanjali's entrepreneurial spirit and commitment to empowering young minds inspires readers of all ages. Students, educators, and parents will learn how to think differently and work more effectively to solve the problems of tomorrow."

—KARLIE KLOSS, Supermodel, Entrepreneur, and Founder of Kode With Klossy

"Gitanjali's book is a delightfully personal, practical, and inspiring *how-to* on STEM innovation and the magic that can transpire when kids are free to embrace failure, think bigger, and dare to make their creative visions a reality. Ever passionate, courageous, and kind, Gitanjali leads by example, sparking a movement for a better and more inclusive tomorrow."

—DR. PARDIS SABETI, Professor, Harvard University, Broad Institute

A Young
Innovator's Guide to
STEM

5 STEPS TO PROBLEM SOLVING
FOR STUDENTS, EDUCATORS,
AND PARENTS

Gitanjali Rao

Post Hill PRESS

A POST HILL PRESS BOOK

A Young Innovator's Guide to STEM:
5 Steps To Problem Solving For Students, Educators, and Parents
© 2021 by Gitanjali Rao
All Rights Reserved

ISBN: 978-1-64293-800-5
ISBN (eBook): 978-1-64293-801-2

Cover art by Cody Corcoran
Interior design and composition by Greg Johnson, Textbook Perfect

Post Hill Press
New York • Nashville
posthillpress.com

Published in the United States of America
3 4 5 6 7 8 9 10

To all my mentors and teachers
who believed in me
and allowed me to fail and learn.

CONTENTS

Welcome ix

Introduction. xi

My Journey. xvi

DISCOVER 1

CHAPTER 1: Science and Our Community—The Higher Purpose 3

CHAPTER 2: What Is Innovation? 10

SOLVE 15

CHAPTER 3: Step 1—Observing 17

CHAPTER 4: Step 2—Brainstorming 26

CHAPTER 5: Step 3—Research 34

CHAPTER 6: Step 4—Building 47

CHAPTER 7: Step 5—Communicating 74

CHAPTER 8: Failing and Iterating 82

IMPLEMENT 87

CHAPTER 9: Spreading Awareness 89

CHAPTER 10: Competing with Your Idea 94

CONCLUSION 116

LESSON PLANS 119

RESOURCES 127

Acknowledgments. 130

About the Author 132

WELCOME

When I first started this journey of innovation, building products, and trying to solve problems around me, I was unsure about what I was doing or why I was going about it in a certain way. There was no clarity of thought on analyzing some problem, classifying the solution approaches, and finally building a solution that was viable; I struggled at every step and never knew what the next step was. While there were several resources on the internet on innovation, there was no straightforward process with clear, handy guidance and a set of tools that I could use to produce an idea-problem-solution combination. It was an exploration each time, and there was no specific direction on ways to seek feedback, find mentors, communicate with experts, get introduced to new technology, and many such things.

While conducting innovation sessions, several students asked me questions that prompted me to think about this deeply.

This is what they asked, and these are very real unknowns for any student:

"How do we do well in school and try to innovate?"

"How do you know which challenge helps learn which skill sets?"

"How do we learn technology in-depth, which we have never been taught in school?"

"How do we know which solution will work?"

"What do your friends in school think about you?"

"There are a lot of ISEF and other STEM challenge winners who have mentioned their journey for inspiration, but how do they do it? We need a prescriptive process and more than just an inspiration."

"Most students think about these only in high school to boost their profile. Why did you start early, when nothing that you do will be counted for your college? Is the time worthwhile?"

"How did your parents help?"

"How do you approach mentors or professors?"

"What is the process you follow that we can reuse?"

There were several other questions, but you get the idea. Many of them wanted me to not just talk to them about their questions but to write them down and send my answers over. I decided to do one better and document all of these responses—and more—in a book. This book, *A Young Innovator's Guide to STEM*, tries to answer all of these questions and also equip a young, inquisitive mind looking to develop innovative solutions, with resources, tools, and tips, to help carve out his or her own journey that is unique to each individual. Coming from somebody roughly their age, my hope is this book will help somebody starting out to visualize their journey, challenge themselves, get out of their comfort zone, and prepare for a future that is unknown to all of us.

INTRODUCTION

Has someone ever told you, "Come up with an idea, any idea at all!"? While that does sound like a lot of fun, it is easy to get stuck trying to think of an idea. Similar to writer's block, people can get innovator's block. What problem do I want to solve? How will I come up with a solution? Why is nothing working? It is a complicated process. A lot of people, especially young innovators like us, try to avoid innovation because they are scared of innovator's block. What I am trying to say is, coming up with ideas is hard. It might take you weeks, months, or even years to come up with the idea that you are proud of. But the important thing is that it is a process—and it is a long one, too. While, yes, it feels like it takes forever, soon you will have an idea that you can make come to life. And with this innovation, you can solve big problems like world hunger, global warming, and cyberbullying. But hey, let's not get too far ahead of ourselves.

Before we start out anything, it is important to understand the reason this book exists and the broad idea of what I am trying to get across. While innovation may seem like another word in the dictionary, it is a combination of some of the things that make up our society. It involves problem-solving, creativity, and the latest developments in technology. Without innovation, I would not be typing up this book. Without innovation, you would not be reading this book.

I want to encourage all of you to think about why you are here and why you want to do this. I want you to imagine the change that you will make in this world. The first step to any innovation process, before we do anything at all, is to go in with a positive mindset. Understand your goals, remember the big picture, and know why you are here. Imagine yourself holding your finished product in your hand, imagine yourself testing it out in remote places, imagine yourself making an impact.

I want to start with a story I am very fond of, which describes this positivity. It was a rainy Tuesday; I was four years old, and I decided I wanted to go on a picnic. I was so disappointed when I looked out the window, and there was rain pouring down, but I decided that I was not going to let that stop me. I was not going to let a drizzle get in my way, so I did not! I picked up my rain boots, a rain hat, my mom's high heels, sunglasses, and an umbrella. I grabbed my basket, and I headed out the door.

I walked a couple of houses down, trying to find the perfect spot for my picnic. I had a massive smile on my face, and I was super excited to sit down, relax, and have the picnic of my life! Before I got the chance to lay out my blanket and open up my basket, I heard the dinnertime call, which meant it was time for me to go home. On the way home, I still had a huge smile on my face, and I was snacking on the chips I had packed for myself.

The reason I told you this story is even though it was raining, even though I was four years old, I knew I wanted to go on a picnic, and I was not going to let anything stop me. I put on a positive attitude and went outside, knowing that I was still going to have fun. I challenge all of you to do the same thing. When you start turning the pages of this book, even if you think you cannot do it or this is too hard for you, look past that! Take this rainy situation and make a picnic out of it.

With that attitude, you can do anything you set your mind to. Take a second to smile even if you are all alone, and nobody can see you and say this aloud, "I can do anything I set my mind to." Say it once or twice, scream it even! I hope that got you pumped up to start reading and exploring. The wonders of innovation are waiting for you.

Who Is This Book For?

In this book, we are going to go through the innovation process and learn the best ways to compete with your ideas with secrets on a slight edge to win. It is a great read for not only students but also families and teachers who want to guide students through an innovation journey.

Students. You will have the chance to read through and discover the spark—or grow the spark already inside of you—to innovate and solve real-world problems, to spread awareness of the problems, and to compete with your solutions. You will have an easy five-step process that you can use to innovate. Not only is this a process that you can use for your projects, but this is something that is repeatable, and you will be able to use it for your other innovation endeavors. Feel free to check out the workspaces at the end of each chapter for some hands-on learning as you understand the fundamentals behind innovation.

Parents. You will have a book full of practical tips and resources to guide your children and help them take their projects from an idea to reality, including popular STEM challenges with timelines to compete and have a slight edge in the competition. Each step consists of a science snapshot, a young innovator looking to make a change in their community. I hope these examples allow your children to think big and think beyond what is ordinary. The end of the book also includes multiple resources for more STEM opportunities, such as camps and events that your children can participate in.

Teachers. Along with the given content, you will find workspaces at the end of each step and lesson plans for each step at the end of the book. The workspaces and lesson plans are specifically tailored towards YOU and YOUR students. It provides not only real-world skills and growth spots for students but also an engaging experience for students of all ages. Each lesson plan includes sections of *Inspire*, *Engage*, and *Immerse*.

This book benefits ANYONE willing to learn, support, and create an innovative future. Here is a quote from Benjamin Franklin that I aimed to model this book after: "Tell me, and I forget, teach me, and I remember, involve me, and I learn." I wanted to write this to involve all of you and make it a fun and engaging experience so that you don't just remember the process—you learn from it and use it every day of your life.

How Do You Read This Book?

The wonderful thing about this journey is that you take it at your own pace. You can take your time with it, and you can go slow, or you can decide on a timeline and try to get through this entire process in three months—from an idea to a well-polished prototype or a real product that you can share with the world. We will learn about new topics, share tips, and even hear about a few examples. This book is split up into three main parts:

Discover—Learn about what innovation *really* is and why you should get excited about it! Dive into the problems we face and learn about some examples in the innovation world! *Discover* intends to be a section where you engage yourself with the world of innovation and find your inner innovator. You will learn about finding your *ikigai* and understanding where to start. You will also be able to *discover* the higher purpose of innovation and why it is a staple in today's society.

Solve—Follow the process to create a solution and solve a real-world problem. Learn about real-world tips and tools that you can use in a prescriptive process. These are the five steps that I hope you will take away with you. *Solve* provides you real-world details about how to go about the process of innovation. Through this process, gather tips, experiences from real youth innovators, and get access to a workspace you can fill out.

Implement—Understand the real meaning behind innovation as a means to help others. Learn how to benefit society with your ideas, spread awareness about the problems you are trying to solve, and even participate in various contests and challenges to receive feedback. Implementation creates a mark on society. It starts a ripple effect with other young innovators in your community. By learning how to implement your ideas and compete with them, make your mark and make a difference.

Then, we will end with a conclusion that motivates you to keep going as well as some resources to explore the world of innovation and competition even more.

Here is a quick guide for what to expect:

 When you see these lightbulbs, these are helpful tips that you can use to navigate your way through the innovation process.

These apples show lesson plans that teachers can use to walk students through the steps of the innovation process in a fun and exciting way.

INTRODUCTION

This is a workspace designed for students/families to monitor progress and challenge yourself. You will also see a QR code that leads to an e-workspace, in case you prefer to work online.

The camera icons give you a "Science Snapshot" of ways other young innovators are exploring the various steps of the process so that you can learn from them!

I want you to take a second and grab a pen and, on this line, right here, write down today's date:

Today's Date: _____

Now, write down your goal end date by which you want to come up with a real product:

End Goal Date: _____

We will come back to the goal date you just wrote down in the conclusion. However, setting a goal for yourself is a great first step to stay motivated and ready to go for what comes ahead.

Last thing! After this, I promise you can start to dive in. As you are reading this book, if you find that you would like more tips and more ideas, please head over to my YouTube channel called "Just STEM Stuff" and the blog that pairs with it. Here is the link: gitanjalijss.blogspot.com. There you will find more innovation tips and a lot more fun activities that you can do!

All right, buckle up! Get out a pencil or a pen, find a comfortable spot to get going. I hope you are excited to start learning new concepts. Welcome to the world of innovation!

MY JOURNEY

I want to start out by telling my story. What I do, why I do it, how I do it, and why I wrote this book. Long story short, I am a science enthusiast and an inventor. I love to come up with new ideas every time I see problems around me.

While I do spend a lot of time in research and solution development, I am like most students my age. I love to bake, take hikes, fence, play the piano, and explore all of my other hobbies. Science and inventing are just another one of them. Chances are if you are reading this book, you really enjoy innovating too, want to try, like to compete, or are working on creating a profile for your high school years that focuses on science and technology.

I come up with some of my best ideas in the most generic places. Sometimes they pop into my brain when I am swimming, pacing around my living room, or even just getting lemonade out of the refrigerator. It's weird, right? But that's exactly what innovation is about. Usually, everything starts to come together when you least expect it.

But anyway, my favorite idea, the one I have been working on for the past five years, and the one that I am *this* close to making a real product, was discovered while I was eating a bowl of pasta on the dinner table after school one day. I know, crazy.

I was nine years old. My parents, my little brother, and I were sitting down at the table, eating some of my dad's famous pasta. Yum! I was shoving pasta down my throat so I could get back to where I left off in a Lego masterpiece. In the background, I heard the news going on like always during dinner. We always liked to have a little bit of background noise as we ate. However, as I twirled some spaghetti around my fork,

something caught my heart. I heard the newscast in the background saying, "Flint, Michigan, is facing a lead in the water crisis…" And that is really all I needed to hear. I turned my complete attention to the TV to see kids my age with mental defects, and it did not feel right.

I immediately asked my parents, "Why are those kids facing so many problems?" My mom, equally worried, replied, "They don't have clean water to drink because there is lead in their drinking water." I started with another question, "What's lead?" This is where my dad jumped in, "Lead is a metal on the periodic table of elements. There was contamination in the pipes in Flint, so lead unexpectedly entered their water and made it poisonous." It seemed unfair. Why do kids like me not have safe water to drink? I took a sip of my cold water and examined it for a bit. I looked at my mom again as my little brother babbled away. I pointed to the glass, "So in Flint, the water I'm drinking right now would have lead in it?" Reluctantly, my mom said yes, as she sucked in some air through her teeth.

I gobbled up my spaghetti and headed to my room. I washed up, brushed, and hopped into my pajamas. I got into bed, but I could barely sleep. I could not stop thinking about everyone who was being affected in Flint. Water is a basic right that everybody should have; it is not a choice.

I woke up the next morning with a new motive in mind. I wanted to do something about the Flint water crisis. I kept that idea in my mind for the longest time but still was not sure how to help.

Little did I know, thinking about the Flint water crisis would change my entire life. One year later, I started by browsing the MIT Tech Review website for hours, looking for technology and ideas that interested me. I learned about things ranging from forensics to space, but the thing that really caught my eye was a new technology called carbon nanotube technology (new at the time). It was then being used to detect food spoilage and harmful gases in the air. I found that so fascinating, so I jotted it down in my journal, but I was not really sure what I was going to do with it. Carbon nanotubes helped with gas, but how did they have ANYTHING to do with water?

I kept looking and learning more about technology like Arduino, 3D printing, electricity, and much more. By the end of the day, I was still stuck. I wasn't able to come up with a solution that used a combination of these ideas. I wanted to solve this problem more than anything, but how?

I spent another week reading, thinking, and pondering upon everything I saw. But I came back to the carbon nanotube idea at the end. Maybe it was something that JUST helped detect gas. But was it really? Could I change it up, so it would work in water as well?

That was my next quest. How could I find a way to make something that dissolves in water super easy, because it is in a powder form, something that can be used in water and be able to detect things in the water? There we went! More reading, researching, and idea-storming. This was not a perfect fairytale where everything happened in the first shot, so... dead end again.

Here is a tip! Do you notice all of these dead ends? This is a normal part of the innovation process! Reaching a final ending is hard, especially when you do not know where you are going with it, but it is important to keep being persistent. You will learn more about this later in the book.

It took me a couple of months to come up with my whole idea of carbon nanotube sensor detection. And by a couple of months, I mean at least three hours a day, seven days a week. It was a really hard process. I had come up with countless ideas in the past, but ideas are much easier than making something a reality.

At the last minute, I actually ended up combining several of the other technologies I heard about because they were so fascinating. The device itself was made out of 3D printing materials, the internal processing system was made out of an Arduino that I learned to code, and the system as a whole is based on the importance of resistance and an electrical current. This was no longer just a chemistry project; it was a STEM project, and I was excited about it.

But...all of this was me dreaming. The actual device looked like a white cardboard box with a hollow back and wires sticking out of it. Doesn't sound so glamorous now, does it? I realized that it was a good idea, but I did not know how to go about making it a reality AT ALL. I wanted feedback and guidance, but I wasn't sure how to get feedback, who to get it from, or at what point in the process to do so. One of my STEM teachers at a 4H club suggested the Discovery Education 3M Young Scientist Challenge to all of us. I decided to submit this idea to the challenge to get a bit more feedback about how I could take this to something more tangible. I had submitted into the challenge a year prior with a different idea and ended up as a state winner. But I really did not feel confident in my new idea, especially because I submitted it just a couple of days before the due date. Most contestants had won science fairs before and had huge poster boards with details on testing, results, and research papers. Here I was, submitting an idea which had an immense potential that I was dreaming about but hadn't yet put much on paper.

It was a waiting game. However, I didn't have to wait for long. To be honest, I kind of forgot about it because I didn't think I had a chance of placing at all, but I kept learning more about water contaminants, how to write code, learning to 3D design, and started solving another problem where astronauts can use a tool to avoid swallowing toothpaste. Sometime in May 2017, I got a call back from the Young Scientist Challenge. I heard the words, "You're one of the top ten finalists of the challenge!" Emotions shifted from my face from something neutral to something excited and even beyond. I was SO excited, I cannot even describe that excitement in words!

This is the best part: I had the opportunity to work with a 3M scientist as my mentor, Dr. Shafer, for three months during the summer. On top of that, my family and I were moving from Nashville, Tennessee, to Lone Tree, Colorado; there was a lot to do. I was terrified of how I was going to get ready for the finals. Most of that summer, I was at the library or in the car while showings for our house were happening when it was on the market. I probably had about two hours every day in the comfort of my own house, and I would take that time to schedule calls with Dr. Shafer and try to work on the solution. When we moved, we were in hotels everywhere, and I still kept going. I longed for the comfort of a home, a place where I did not live on the minimal things we had in suitcases. By the time I moved to our new home, it was time for a new school. The disruption of moving actually motivated me to keep working on the real solution to the water crisis whenever I got a few hours. When I was sitting, just waiting to get into my new house, I would read articles about every Flint individual and what they went through. This gave me a perspective of why this was a critical issue, and I wanted to bring awareness to the problem of lead in contaminated water. I did a lot of reading and reached out to local water organizations to learn more about this issue, which gave me EVEN MORE motivation to keep going.

I started getting into the technology portion of things. I reached out to nanomaterial manufacturers to get samples of carbon nanotubes based on my specifications and ended up requesting tours of the place. I picked up the phone only to end up with COUNTLESS cold calls to chemistry professors to get feedback on my idea. Everything I did had only one motivation, and that was to try and fix the real issue. I was confused as to what I was doing. It was utter and complete chaos in my head because I learned a lot more about the problem and the people who had to suffer through it.

Dr. Shafer helped me take a breath of fresh air and realize, "We need to focus on the solution, and we can do this, I CAN do this." And I did… three months later, I was on my way to St. Paul, Minnesota, to compete in the YSC finals with nine other AMAZING kids for three days. I was pumped up, nervous, but mostly excited.

At the airport, I was shocked at myself and the progress I had made. Wow…three months of me coming up with my own solutions and finally coming up with a completed solution. But thinking back to it, it was never really my first completed idea/solution, although it seemed like it. Ever since I was in second grade, I had been actively inventing and coming up with ideas that I found a personal interest in. I worked on space-saving chairs on space shuttles and space stations that fold into the floor once astronauts are done using them, devices to reduce the effect of allergies due to airborne pollen using electrostatic fields, an airplane Blackbox detector to find missing planes using underwater laser communication, and another device to help with early diagnosis of snake bites using non-contact thermography. Building such devices and solving problems has always interested me, but I did not exactly see that I had always been interested in innovation until the moment I was getting ready to board the plane for the finals. I had just thought those ideas I was coming up with were something that I would do in my free time before my other after-school activities. I never really looked at it as something that was special. I heard our flight boarding and continued to follow that thought. I was innovating for years now, and this was the first time I was making one of my ideas an actual reality. I'm proud that the years of solving problems had become a habit and that I was recognized for one of my ideas. I was ready to go, and I was so excited about the week ahead.

When I finally got there, I participated in a set of onsite challenges, met others interested in the same things I am, FINALLY got to meet Dr. Shafer and NOT over Skype, and finally presented my idea to a panel of judges and a lot of other people. It was intimidating, but one of the best experiences of my life. I learned a lot from my peers, who were all older than me. Going into the day of the banquet where they announced the winner, I was not sure who was going to win, but I was glad that I brought to fruition something that had just been an idea. I knew that, no matter what the results of the competition were, I wanted to take my water contamination innovation further because I felt connected to several Flint residents through my research. I had gained self-confidence that I could request mentors to guide me. I was only eleven at the time, and I had learned that it is fine to discuss my simple ideas with distinguished scientists and professors. Four months before that moment, I had been terrified to talk to Dr. Shafer virtually because I was not sure what she would think of me. But with the help of Dr. Shafer, I learned the discipline of following a process, having a deadline, and committing to what I was creating. Unfortunately, on the night of the banquet,

Dr. Shafer had to be somewhere else due to her work commitments. However, as I waited for the results of the competition, I reflected on my journey myself. I was sitting there thinking, "What can I do next? Can I visit Flint? Can I influence Federal Laws about water quality testing? Who can I partner with to help make this a REAL product?"

My parents and my mentor were proud of me for presenting in front of an audience on a subject that professors would have taken years to master. My friends at the challenge had equally amazing ideas, presentations, and plans. I was more excited than nervous to hear the result.

We sat through the speeches and remarks as the suspense was built up. When they started to ramp up to the winner, my heart was beating out of my chest. To my surprise, they announced ME—MY NAME, GITANJALI RAO. This was a totally new experience for me. My mind was dizzy. There were so many people, and it took me a second to process it. After I processed it (WOW! was I excited!), that feeling of going up on stage was AMAZING, and it was definitely the moment that changed my life forever. As I was walking to the stage after they called my name, there was one thing clear in my head: I could not stop here. The process I used worked well and there should be more of me developing innovative solutions. All I needed was a place to start, a spark, and, most importantly, a way to describe the process that focused on innovation so that it is repeatable and can be shared with everybody. I was just eleven, but I felt a sense of responsibility to share my experience with others. If I had to go through the innovation process again, I knew exactly where to start, what to do, and what not to do. I could eliminate unnecessary fears and approach the innovation process with confidence.

While I have now shared with you a big part of what *I* did, I cannot emphasize enough the effort of my parents, who have been so supportive along my journey.

I was always a very shy student. At about the age of four, my mom started putting me in uncomfortable situations such as museum camps, where I had to meet other students that were much older than me. I remember my mom dropping me off on the doorsteps of a science camp and letting me know that I should trust her because she would never put me in a situation that was unsafe. I would go inside with tears in my eyes, but as soon as we started our activities, I was excited and wanted to do more.

It soon became a routine. My mom would put me in the next uncomfortable thing, and slowly I stretched myself without even knowing I was doing it. The same went with my knowledge. My mom would mentor a group of students from my class for a national STEM challenge. In the first year I participated, in second grade, we just had sketches of our basic idea. The year after, we created a website, and then after that, we created a video of our proposed solution to the problem we wanted to tackle. Every year our skills were growing without us realizing that we were learning something new.

Speaking of mentorship, my parents introduced concepts to me in a fun and interesting way. I remember when I was five or six years old, my parents always gave me a problem, and I was given three minutes to come up with a few ideas to solve the problem and present it to them in a clear and concise manner. My mom was usually my competitor, and my dad was the judge. My dad would present an impromptu problem to create an "innovative restaurant." We would present, and we were judged on our communication, creativity, technology, and user experience. I used to have a blast coming up with the presentation in three minutes. It was thrilling, and I always wanted to do more. I always ended up winning, and the prize was a big hug, a homemade certificate, or a trip to the ice-cream store. We used to play this on road trips as well. Once my brother was born, we continued this game. As the reigning champion, I was so eager to have another competitor. Little did I know, my title would be lost. My brother now wins, my mom and I still compete, and my dad is still the judge. At the time, it was just a silly game, but problem-solving, innovating, and building solutions became a habit for me.

I loved patterns and learning by visually seeing things, so my parents always taught me all math concepts using patterns. I was taught science concepts like rocks by actually feeling different types of rocks or intestine functions by putting red jelly in a tube. I was introduced to all the helping verbs in a song format to a *"Frère Jacques"* tune.

My brother loves mythology, and we teach him decimals by showing him how his favorite Indian god Ganesh, which is the decimal, moves right or left depending on whether he has multiplied by tens or divided by tens of thousands. When he was four, he learned the basics of addition by showing him Egyptian hieroglyphic characters. He learned the

concept of "PEMDAS" (or order of operations in math) using Egypt's hierarchical structure.

My parents let us dream big, and that is the reason I am here, writing this book. My parents shared every tool that they used in their professional environment with me so that I got a feel of what they do and how adults work together, whether it is the stages of teamwork, feasibility analysis, or business models. As they introduced me to these, I internalized all of it and started trying it myself for my process of innovation. If you take a closer look, some of the tools used in this book are all from professional settings that organizations use.

There you go, that is my journey, and what started out with recognition and interviews has led up to this book and more in the future. The process that you will read here is what I use for absolutely everything I come up with and every challenge I participate in.

At the same time, I started a product "Epione," a device that diagnoses prescription opioid addiction, as well as "Kindly," a service that detects and prevents cyberbullying. This was the start of a new journey where I was motivated to see more, do more, and be more.

While I have shared my story with you, I want each one of YOU to write your OWN story. I want to share with you what innovation is, why you should be excited about it, how to go about it, how to win with it, how to share your journey with others, and, most of all, how to bring awareness to everyday problems and influence decisions. Each and every one of us can be equipped for the unknown future and draft our own story.

Coming Up Next

We talked about how the book is organized and my personal story that drove towards sharing what I learned. In the coming chapters, we will get right into the thick of things where I would like to walk you through the process of innovation. As mentioned earlier, I have organized the process into three broad categories that we all identify with so that they are practical and easier to comprehend. These are "DISCOVER," "SOLVE," and "IMPLEMENT."

We start with the DISCOVER section that digs into the background of innovation, specifically scientific innovation, and the role it has and continues to play in transforming our lives. The two chapters in the section are to highlight the role and need for innovation and the importance of solving the problems that ail many among us. While innovation for the sake of innovation is fine, this section tries to show why it should also have a higher purpose of alleviating the daily challenges we face around the world. At the end of the second chapter, I would also like to introduce my five-step process for innovation.

So, let us get right into it.

DISCOVER

"The true laboratory is the mind,
where behind illusions we uncover the laws of truth."

—JAGADISH CHANDRA BOSE

This section of the book goes over the reasons behind what innovation is and why we should be excited about it! Learn about the history behind it and your first steps into it.

CHAPTER 1

Science and Our Community— The Higher Purpose

Ikigai. I was never really one for pithy aphorisms like "you can create your own future" or terms in exotic languages defining life's purpose. However, for many reasons that I may not be fully able to explain, the term "ikigai" stayed with me. "Ikigai" is a Japanese idea that means "a reason for living." As someone who is fond of the cultural impact of global ideas, I took it upon myself to learn more about it. Wanting to know more, I made it my goal to discover what my ikigai is. What I love to do, what I want to do, what my passion is, and what MY reason for living is.

Discovering my ikigai has not been a straightforward path. I sat down at my desk with a notebook and a pen. I wrote down what I love to do. I wrote down things ranging from riding bikes to reading books, from hanging with my friends to baking. I looked at the list, knowing

something was off. Books and baking did not truly define me, and it was not really capturing my flavor. They were more like the cover to the book of me rather than the chapters that explain what I do, how I live, and my aspirations. I realized it was going to be a much longer journey than one rainy Tuesday with a notebook.

Now, why am I telling you this story? The moral is you have to learn what makes you, you! What makes you unique, different, and YOUR reason for being. After three extensive years of learning who I am, I found my ikigai. I am not just an innovator; I promote ideas and I use science as a catalyst for social change to help spread my knowledge globally. My passion for outreach and stressing the importance of youth in innovation is MY ikigai. Before we get back to this concept, let us talk about innovation.

Why do we have to innovate or develop solutions? We do not have to, but we need to understand why it is important for us to solve problems. We are growing in a world where problems that did not exist fifty years ago are now dominant. Things like global warming and climate changes, adolescent depression, contamination of our natural resources, uncontrolled population growth, pandemics, internet security, long-distance space travel, and cyberbullying—just to name a few—are part of our daily life, and each has their own set of problems.

I am writing this book during the COVID-19 pandemic. I do not think this is the last time we are going to see a pandemic in this world. Things we took for granted, such as going to school, hanging out with our friends, and shopping, have changed forever. Questions are constantly running through my mind. Is there a faster way to produce vaccinations? Is there a better way to do contact tracing and immediate quarantine? Are there better and cheaper nano filters and microbeads that kill viruses faster?

It is our generation's responsibility to do something about all or any of it. It may not be solving all of it, but it is at least understanding our responsibility to identify what these problems are, how we can help, and how to bring awareness so actions are taken. The good news is we are not short of problems. For example, there was no federal law for testing lead in drinking water in most states when I started thinking about Tethys. But understanding the water contamination problem and talking about it can make a difference, and it did. Universities and individuals in India, Brazil, and other countries invested in research on nanomaterials for environmental testing after the news on Tethys. Now, I see several research papers on the same. Did I influence them directly? I am not sure, but they are all taking a step in the right direction. So, what does it tell us? We can influence lawmakers, universities, organizations, and decision-makers by starting SOMEWHERE.

Your first reaction may be, "These are complicated and complex issues. I will never solve problems by myself." I assure you, solving problems does not mean you have to have a Ph.D. or be an extremely gifted student. Let us go back to that idea of ikigai. If you are able to find your ikigai, all you need is your determination and passion. Do not rush the process, take your time, and understand who you want to be. Your ikigai can be implemented in the innovation process and can help you connect with the process even more. When I introduced this concept, one girl told me that her ikigai was being creative and sharing her art with other people.

Did you know you can solve problems using art? For example, Origami—the Japanese art of paper folding—is actively researched to design compact solar panels that travel to Mars and unfold on arrival.

Here are some more:

- **Problem**: Maybe your community or school does not recycle despite having recycling bins.
- **Solution:** You can create a poster with your art or create a super-hero with your talent and share it with students and teachers or request the principal to send it out monthly to create awareness.

Another young boy told me that his ikigai, even though he was not clear on it yet, was finding a way to help others using the world of sports and soccer.

Well, how can we help others with soccer?

- **Problem:** You are working on a project with your team members at school, but you do not seem to mesh or trust each other at all.
- **Solution:** Go out to a soccer field and practice creating game-plays. Spend an hour playing with each other, gaining trust, and learning the work ethic of everyone.

While science and technology are valuable means, I personally feel learning should also focus on "kindness." Empathy and consideration of others help us understand problems better and can motivate people to help others. If we are learning applied structural engineering, we need to know about communities that have structural issues due to natural disasters and how we can help them. Whether it is science or geography or physics, innovation should start with how we can apply societal changes, culture, and distribution to improve health or economy. If we learn science, it should be about how we can apply these concepts to solve problems.

While I just shared a couple of examples, the aim of this book is to use science and technology as a catalyst for social change. Students in general, like you and me, are like sponges and can learn what is shared with us in a fun and entertaining manner. Not everything can be taught by classwork or taking a test or the idea of getting an "A+." We deserve an education where we are allowed to fail and learn with hands-on problem-solving. So, let us try this out together and bring about a movement. The only person who can stop us now is ourselves.

Recently, I was part of a global power summit, which focused on the role of science and harnessing youth ingenuity for sustainable living. Greta Thunberg started the movement for climate action, and her voice urged everyone to "listen to science." What does that mean when we say "listen to science?" It means understanding the facts and figures to comprehend the problem better. It also means looking for ways to solve problems and bringing awareness to them. When we refer to the UN's Sustainable Development Goals (SDGs), we will know that we have come a long way but still have a long way to go to maintain our future.

Along those lines, we need to come together to show the world what youth can do. We need to BE the change; we need to create that change and watch it define our future and create a ripple effect amongst other young innovators across the planet. Find your ikigai, find your passion, be that change, and help the world. No matter their age, gender, race, etc., anybody can be an innovator, and anyone can produce ideas. We do not need expensive equipment, living in select cities, or having the best labs to start solving problems. All we need is an intention and commitment to make it happen. For me personally, with the limited resources I have, most times, it is easier to tackle a smaller subset of a problem that has more impact, and I have a better chance of managing the scope.

Girls in Stem

I wanted to talk a bit here about being a girl in STEM and start by sharing another personal story. A few years back, I was very excited to join a STEM lab program. I wanted to meet new friends and learn new topics. However, the result was seven boys and me, who ended up being part of the club. Instantly, my unconscious mind created a bias that maybe I do not belong here. After the lesson, I realized this is what I love to do, and at that moment, it didn't matter to me who I was with. This happened one other time when I joined a coding camp while I was in third grade. I was the only girl throughout the week of summer camp, and the end project was to create a game. When my teammates and I started creating the game, they started with just boy characters. I asked them to add girls, and they were apologetic that they forgot. It is not that they did that intentionally. They just didn't think of anybody else who didn't look like them or act as they did.

Was I affected because I was surrounded by boys? Yes, at first, but not at the end.

Did I feel like I didn't fit in? I didn't worry about what others thought, and I didn't find a difference.

Did I still enjoy the topics I learned about, the games I created, and the experiments I performed? Yes, of course.

I want to bring across the message and importance of girls in STEM. If there is one thing I want to change in our society, it would be to ensure that girls are provided safe spaces to pursue STEM. Research shows that girls don't necessarily get into STEM for the same reasons that boys get into STEM. While both want to understand the purpose behind what they are doing and why they are doing it, most girls usually like to see more art and creativity in the space they work rather than robots and machinery with actions. In my interview with some of my friends, who are girls, they like to approach STEM creatively, incorporating art, music, and community services compared to my friends who are boys. When I listened to them explain this to me, I asked my mom if she saw a difference in how my brother and I approached problem-solving. She had a very similar thought where my brother would spend a few minutes to understand a problem and rushed to provide a creative solution and then work backwards to see if it solved it. While I would spend more time on the problem, draw the features, and ask for feedback before coming up with solutions. Together we made a great team. There is nothing wrong with either approach. A collaborative approach would bring the best result.

There are many reasons why girls tend to stay away from STEM careers compared to boys. But I have narrowed it down to five, whether it is young girls or grown-up women:

1. **Isolation:** Most of us girls have been in coding camps or STEM camps where we may be the only one or two. While this has improved over the last several years, this is still prevailing. I have friends who do not want to try coding and have no good reason other than the fact that they believe it is not for them.

2. **Lack of Encouragement:** In my elementary school, I remember that girls were encouraged to join the American Girl Doll clubs, and flyers were provided. I didn't even know such a thing existed! If the same thing was done for coding or STEM clubs and it was targeted to girls, I believe there would have been several of us who would have joined.

3. **Media Portrayal:** Every science video we are or were introduced to usually has boys or men portrayed as scientists. The local library, which has science shows, usually had men explaining the science concepts. I never placed myself in their shoes until I received some recognition. I believe we have the opportunity to change this.

4. **Responsibility:** Women in professional settings in STEM careers are not entrusted with greater responsibilities due to the belief that their personal responsibilities for their families at home might interfere with their work. Things have changed recently, but it continues to persist in pockets. Regardless, employers need to provide equal opportunities to all employees, with decisions on responsibilities made solely based on the talent and ability to perform the job.

5. **The Wage Gap:** While I was in 6th grade, I worked on a bill for a local Youth in Government program about the need to end the wage gap where women get eighty cents for every dollar a man gets. It was appalling when I first heard of it, and when my mother explained the reasons behind it, it was very unfair. This is still

prevailing in many industries, including STEM careers. Employers need to follow laws on not asking for previous salaries, stop repercussions for discussing salaries among employees, and provide an equal salary structure for a given position with no room for negotiation.

Attracting and retaining more women in the STEM workforce will maximize innovation and creativity. Scientists and engineers are working to solve some of the most difficult challenges of our time. There are women pioneers who have immensely contributed to science. Whether it is Marie Curie and her discovery of two elements or Emmanuelle Charpentier and Jennifer Doudna for inventing gene editing using the CRISPR technique, science has made huge leaps due to the efforts of women. When women or girls are not involved in STEM, our experiences, needs, and desires that are unique to us may be overlooked, and solutions will not have our representation. It is our responsibility to ensure all of us are treated the same in the future. While we girls can involve ourselves more in STEM, it is equally the responsibility of adults and boys to ensure they speak up for us and respect our skills. I am thankful to several organizations that are providing a safe space for girls to try STEM skills. However, it is equally important for young girls to take a personal interest and initiative in STEM fields. The problems of today and tomorrow need all of us to solve.

CHAPTER 2

What Is Innovation?

Do we really know what innovation is? I bet you have heard the word on the news or heard businesses say it. It is one of those words that you think you know, but you actually realize, "Oh wait, do I actually know this?" Innovation is the process of improving or enhancing existing processes or tools together to solve a problem. It is like organized chaos, but innovation is what you make out of it.

Let us talk about something that might sound similar—the scientific method. Essentially, it goes through the process of finding a question, creating a hypothesis, testing the hypothesis, compiling data, coming up with a conclusion, and doing it all over again. This is something I learned in school and thought was pretty cool. It made my life easier when performing an experiment and when I came to a conclusion. But I wanted more. I wanted to know what to do with that conclusion. The scientific process answers your questions; the innovation process helps you use those answers to help yourself, the world, or even put a smile on someone's face. Little do you know, you use both every day. Whether it is contemplating whether to warm up a pizza in the microwave or an oven or creating ground-breaking technology, you are thinking of innovative ideas, answering your questions, and implementing them.

If you are like me and want definitions to write down, this is what innovation is:

The process of enhancing, building, and learning something new to solve a problem.

Now you can decide what you want to build and learn! But there is a keyword in that definition, and it is *process*. In this book, it is all about process, Process, PROCESS! We are going to work through the process of innovation together, and then you can take it to whatever heights you want. Later, we will discuss some of the ways that you can compete and get that slight edge to get feedback, grants, or scholarships. While going through the process together, you may come across existing project management or professional tools. I repurposed these for all of us to understand and make use of. Fishbone diagrams, affinity diagrams, and matrices, just to name a few, are used by adults in their professional settings daily, but it was an "aha" moment when I tried to use it for the innovation process. I never understood why concepts like these were not necessarily taught in school. But I have decided to put it into action.

Let us throw another concept here. First, decide: are you going to *invent* or *innovate?* This defines EVERYTHING. The difference between inventing and innovating is:

Inventing—Defining an idea from scratch, building something from bottom to the top, or the introduction of a process for the first time.

Innovating—Using existing technology and building upwards to solve more problems and improving the current solutions that are out there.

I have found that innovating gets me to my results quicker, more effectively, and gives me a lot of room for creativity. Inventing, on the other hand, is AMAZING if you have an original idea, but it makes it easier to get stuck under a block. It is up to you, but I want to focus more on using our background knowledge and building up from a foundation. This is a common mistake young innovators make: If it is hard to *invent* something, *innovate* something. Slowly, you can turn your innovation into an invention as you learn the reasoning behind why you are doing what you are doing.

For this to work for both of us, there's a couple of rules to follow:

- This process is just a guide. Before you reach the end of this book, make one change to the process so that you make it special to you and *only* you.

- Do not feel pressured to come up with an idea on your first try. Think of a chicken (weird analogy) when they lay an egg, it can take a while to hatch. An idea can take FOREVER to hatch. The trick is to be patient. It will hatch eventually, I promise. You do not have to put hard deadlines on you, but the trick is to think about it everywhere you go and during everything you do.
- Come up with your own set of tools if the one in this book is tough to understand or make use of. Another place to use innovation!

We will go through these in detail. To make it easy, I like you to think of the process using a mnemonic:

Old Bananas Regularly Belong in Cake

This helps me remember the process. Now, if we take the first letter of each of those words, voila! We have our process in five steps.

Step 1: O—Observe
Step 2: B—Brainstorm
Step 3: R—Research
Step 4: B—Build
Step 5: C—Communicate

Each of these different steps is important in their own distinct way, and we will be talking in-depth about every single one of these.

To give you a brief overview, observing sounds like an extremely broad term, which it is! *Step 1: Observing* is the way that you can find problems that you want to solve and questions that you want to answer. For me personally, this is one of the hardest steps of the innovation process, but taking walks, watching the news, reading magazine articles, and even just being observant might give you ideas that you never thought about and help you narrow those ideas down.

Next stop! *Step 2: Brainstorming.* When I first started to make this process, I thought brainstorming was the step that you needed to come up with a final idea. Little did I know, I was SO wrong. Brainstorming is just giving you a chance to jot down everything in your notebook and start labeling them. At this step, there is no such thing as a bad idea.

Next, we have *Step 3: Researching!* Research is a terrifying term. Scrolling through hundreds and hundreds of web pages...spending days in the library...collecting a lot of magazines. While this may sound monotonous, it is much more fun than it sounds once we stay a bit longer on it. Research simply means coming up with a cool idea. Later in the book, you will learn about the correct and proper way to conduct research as well. Research is about narrowing down your brainstormed list to the ideas that have potential by using various tools such as matrices.

Next, we have *Step 4: Building!* My personal favorite. We are going to be talking more in-depth about building in Chapter 7, but the reason I think of building as one of my favorite steps is it gives you a visual demonstration of your project/idea. For example, when I was building my device, Tethys, the first thing I did was build a prototype! Yes, it was not the most beautiful thing in the world, but it got the job done. I then knew what I wanted my device to look like, even though the model was made out of cardboard. Do not get discouraged when your first prototype does not look exactly how you want it to look. Because I guarantee you, if you keep trying and persevering, it will look even better than you want it to look!

Finally, we have *Step 5: Communicating!* I enjoy this step a lot. I am communicating my ideas right now with all of you. Communicating can be tricky and sometimes even frightening, but it is important to address that once you have come up with an awesome idea, you need to show the world what you have done. Communicating can come in so many different forms: a book, a speech, a demonstration, an art piece, a video, or even an interpretive dance. The possibilities are endless.

Coming Up Next

Hopefully, you are well-grounded about the motivations and the need for innovation. We also talked a bit about the innovation process in this chapter. The next section is "SOLVE," where across six chapters, we go deeper into the process and each of the steps involved. I have dedicated a chapter in this section for each of the five steps in the process, plus an additional chapter on the importance of learning through failure. Confidence of success is always great, but we sometimes get so mentally invested in the success that we are not really prepared for the inevitable failure we are bound to experience in the journey. I thought it would be good to share my lessons from failure and how you can learn from them and commit a few mistakes. The five steps themselves are prescriptive, with detailed examples. Each of the steps has a workspace at the end of the chapter that you can use to understand the step better and even use them for your own project. The workspace is yours to fill in any way you want, and I strongly suggest you use the templates for practice and your projects. For teachers and educators, I have included lesson plans in one of the later sections of the book that you can use with your students for each of the innovation steps. They worked great for me down the years, and I am hopeful you will benefit from them.

Let us dive into the process, innovators!

SOLVE

"It always seems impossible until it's done."

—NELSON MANDELA

This section of the book helps you understand how to think creatively and walks you through my innovation process. Come up with tons of ideas, narrow them down, and build in ways you never thought possible to evolve your ideas!

CHAPTER 3

Step 1—Observing

I asked a group of kindergartners the broad question of "What do you like?" Some said cars, some plants, some animals, and I asked them to look for their favorite things and observe them for a week. Then, they wrote down everything they found and thought would be a problem people might face. It was amazing to see what they came up with. One little boy said, "Cars are great, they come in assorted colors, shapes, and they can be self-driving too, but accidents can still happen!" Another little girl said, "I love plants, but the flowers from a lot of plants have a lot of pollen, and my dad gets allergies in spring because of the flowering plants." In a week, the whole group came up with tons of problems that could be solved.

Before we start anything, I want you to think back to what YOU like. What you like to do, what you like to see, what you like to play with, anything. If it is something you are passionate about, it helps you get through the process of innovation. So, take a second to think about some things that you like and have them in your brain.

Seeing the world around us can lead to some amazing ideas and help you identify the problems that you want to solve. In this chapter, we will discuss the basics of how to look for problems, narrow down problems, and identify a problem to stick with.

Looking for Problems

The first roadblock in the innovation process is usually coming up with a problem that you want to solve. It was one of the hardest parts of the process for me, but since then, I have learned to work around it. I really want to describe and help you through the process of observing. We will be using a variety of different tools and methods to make the process as easy as possible for you.

Let us start out with the point of observing. Observing helps you come up with and connect to problems that you see around you. You can learn about problems or serious issues by looking at:

- News
- Magazines
- Books
- Websites
- And many more…

You can draw inspiration from anything. You do not even need to know what you are looking for. I want to focus today on learning about how to draw inspiration from going outside. I know that seems a little bit unconventional. However, going outside is one of the best ways that I like to come up with ideas and learn about problems.

Let us take a breather and go outside on a quick walk. Now that you are outside, I want you to take a second and write down or think about three things that you never noticed before. It could be a birdhouse in your neighbor's tree or even some fresh flowers blooming. **I notice...**

Now, look for three things that you are confused about. This might seem difficult, but it could be something you are curious about, you have questions about, or you just identify as problematic. For me, some of the sidewalk squares are starting to crack around our house! **I wonder...**

Lastly, I want you to write down or think about one thing in your neighborhood you would like to explore more! This could be one of the three things you are confused about or something else; it is YOUR innovation journey, so it is up to you!

The goal of something like this is just to help you explore more.

I hope that gave you a great understanding of what it is like to come up with questions and problems. For Tethys, I drew my inspiration from seeing a little creek on a walk and exploring more about what is in our water. I then came across the Flint Water Crisis. For Epione, the device I created to diagnose prescription opioid addiction, we were driving down the highway and remembered a family friend of ours who faced a car accident and got addicted to prescription opioids. For Kindly, the artificial intelligence service I created to detect cyberbullying phrases, I drew inspiration from my school and others around the world where students face cyberbullying. However, those are just a few examples. I encourage you to use this process to come up with problems that you would like to solve.

Here is a tip! Remember that one thing you would like to explore more? We are going to continue along with that idea throughout the rest of this book in the workspaces, so make sure to have something you are really interested in!

Narrowing Down Problems

Let us start by breaking down your problem or question. This step allows us to take a broader question or idea and break it up into smaller parts. To do this, we are going to use a common technique called a fishbone diagram, also known as the Ishikawa diagram. I repurposed this commonly used tool for analyzing the root cause of problems to something we can use for narrowing the problem domain and identifying a problem that we can realistically aim to develop a solution for. The purpose here of a fishbone diagram is to identify the most common causes of your main problem categorized under equipment, process, environment, and people. These causes now help us to narrow the problem we want to address. Here is a template of a fishbone diagram:

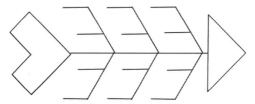

As we can see, it almost looks like the bone structure of a fish. *Hence* we can remember the term fishbone diagram! Here are the divisions of the fishbone diagram:

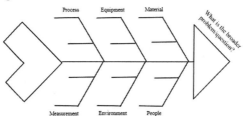

To provide a real-world example, here is the fishbone diagram I created for Tethys, so I knew which branch of the problem I wanted to solve.

💡 **Here is a tip!** Note that I did not use all the bones of the fish. I did not NEED to use all the bones. I only used the ones that made sense for me to use. If you need more or fewer bones, go for it. It is up to you!

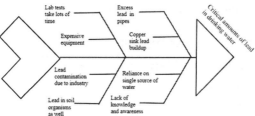

This should not be an exact replica of what your fishbone diagram looks like; therefore, feel free to have one, two, or even three or more ideas on each bone. Soon after, I realized that the branch that I wanted to take a deeper look at was the lack of knowledge or awareness of lead contamination in drinking water. But how exactly did I do that with these many probable causes?

Science Snapshot! Meet Julia Gelfond. After getting her four baby molars pulled, she saw that the resulting holes that were left in the gum were painful, easily irritated, and could get infected. To tackle this problem, Julia created an innovative dissolvable gel that can fill a tooth hole after the tooth has been extracted to ensure that further complications do not arise.

Identifying a Problem

Once I had a group of problems that contributed to my core problem, I used a technique quite common in business classes called a 2x2 matrix. I like to call this the 4-square method. While this is not the only way, it is effective in giving a clear visual representation of your decision process.

The 4-square method involves four different sections to find out which idea is "just right." Here is a model for you to check out.

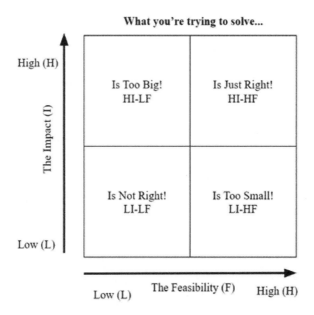

What you're trying to solve...

High (H)	Is Too Big! HI-LF	Is Just Right! HI-HF
Low (L)	Is Not Right! LI-LF	Is Too Small! LI-HF

The Impact (I)

Low (L)   The Feasibility (F)   High (H)

Now, take a few minutes to sort out the ideas you thought of during the fishbone process into the 4-square. Try not to do any research at this point. You want to go with your original gut to tell you where each of these might belong based on your background knowledge. YOUR knowledge can help you understand if you can make your idea a reality. When you have it sorted out, look at that green box. Those are the ideas you want to go after. I will take a second to explain the reasoning behind it.

You want to make it your main goal to balance out impact and feasibility. Obviously, we want to solve a problem with high impact, but also, we want to make sure that it is actually feasible to solve it that way. That is what leads up to that green box to choose from. Here is my 4-square for Tethys:

What you're trying to solve...

	Low (L) — The Feasibility (F) — High (H)	
High (H)	Expensive equipment Is Too Big! HI-LF Fumes lead to further pollution — Children health issues	Is Just Right! HI-HF Lack of knowledge of lead in drinking water
Low (L)	Lab tests take lots of time Is Not Right! LI-LF Excess lead pipes	Copper sink lead buildup Is Too Small! LI-HF Lead in soil organisms as well

(The Impact (I): High (H) to Low (L); The Feasibility (F): Low (L) to High (H))

The smaller font shows my ideas that might seem familiar because I developed them using the fishbone diagram. I then used the 4-square to break them down, and voila! I realized that the problem that was "just right" for me was looking more at the lack of knowledge of lead in drinking water.

💡 **Here is a tip!** If you do end up with a couple of problems in the green box, try using the further questions to narrow the problems down or find a unique way to combine your ideas so you can create a mega-solution that can solve multiple problems!

However, as I mentioned earlier, my 4-square method is only one of the ways to narrow down the problem. While I like to start there, we must recognize that there are several other factors that contribute to the eventual decision of which problem to tackle. The following are some other criteria that are equally important in weighing the best problem to address, in addition to the conclusions of my 4-square analysis.

1. Is your problem worthwhile? Even though it has a high impact, and it is very feasible, do people want it, or will a solution be used? Is someone already working on a solution to this, or has somebody already tried it before? Also, can we really solve the problem, or are we looking at a temporary fix? Can people afford a product or a solution? Is the solution more challenging to adopt than living with the problem?

2. Is your problem timely? This allows you to gauge the time at which you want to solve this problem. Do you see this as a problem that people are still facing? Is it outdated, or is it something that has not made an enormous impact yet? Sometimes statistics might not be correct or are outdated. What seemed like an impactful solution might currently have limited use.

3. Does your problem spark further research? I like to ask myself this question. A good problem, even after solved, should be able to spark curiosity and allow people to do further research on it. Some of the greatest problems or questions—for example, the theory of evolution—were created with layers and different people.

Do not just limit yourself to these tools and ideas! Observing is a theoretical step. It is not a step where you should mathematically decide which problem works best for you. You can use tools to point you in the right direction, but all of these deciding factors are unique to YOU, YOUR goal, and YOUR mission.

Coming Up Next

In this step, we observed the problem, narrowed it down to something we felt had the most impact, and selected one to pursue. In the next step, we will look at the solution space. We will learn some techniques and look at tools to dig deeper into the problem, research our problem further, and organize our solution ideas.

Step 1: Observe Workspace

Please follow along with your teachers as you use this workspace to go through the observing process. Follow the numbers next to each activity/diagram in chronological order.

1. Fishbone Diagram

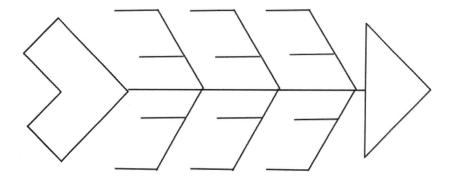

2. 4-Square

What you're trying to solve...

	Low (L) — High (H)	
High (H)	Is Too Big! HI-LF	Is Just Right! HI-HF
Low (L)	Is Not Right! LI-LF	Is Too Small! LI-HF

The Impact (I)

Low (L)   The Feasibility (F)   High (H)

3. Confirmation Questions

Is your problem worthwhile?

_____

If your answer is no, how can you make it more worthwhile?

_____

_____

Is your problem timely?

_____

_____

If your answer is no, how can you make it timelier?

_____

_____

Does your problem spark further research?

_____

If your answer is no, how can you make it spark further research?

_____

_____

After your analysis, what is the problem you choose to solve? Why?

_____

_____

_____

_____

_____

_____

CHAPTER 4

Step 2—Brainstorming

Brainstorming. A word that I like to say is commonly used but not necessarily understood. Do you remember around the beginning of this book, when I said, "Do we really know what innovation is? I bet you have heard it on the news or heard businesses say it. It is one of those words that you think you know, but you realize, 'Oh wait, do I actually know this?'" In my eyes, I think the same applies to the process of brainstorming. We are going to practice the idea of individual brainstorming.

Initial Research

While we are not at the research step yet, it is super beneficial to do a little bit of initial research at the beginning of the brainstorming process. Since we are jumping directly from a problem to a solution, I think it is important to find a way to understand and connect to the issue. Try looking at basic articles online or even contacting people you know to find the answers to these questions:

- Who are the victims of the problem that you plan to solve?
- How are the victims emotionally and physically impacted?
- If you had a solution to the problem, how would they feel?
- Apart from the victims, who else is impacted indirectly? Government, children, teens, certain demographics, offices, schools, etc.
- What are some statistics about the issue?
- What is the history of this issue?

This is just a guide for potential questions you can ask. Keep learning, keep looking up, and searching through things to get a better understanding of the problem you want to solve. Now that you might have found a connection or realized the true impact, you might have some ideas already circulating in your head. But, before we write them down, think about this list too:

- What solutions currently exist to solve the problem?
- Are there any gaps in the current solutions that can be filled?
- Are there any breakthrough technologies that are being looked at to solve this problem?

Current solutions are a particularly important part of defining a solution. You can look at what has already been done out there to either build upon existing solutions or create something even better. We will use this very extensively in the "Researching" chapter. Found a lot of current solutions that people are using effectively and have minimal gaps? You might have to go back to observing and to your list of problems.

Here is a tip! Innovation is an iterative process, so there might be several steps where you feel lost. It is OKAY. That's part of the process. It will get easier as you go along! We will talk about this more in detail in the "Failing and Iterating" chapter, and I will provide some resources about "A Growth Mindset" under "Resources."

A List of Ideas

Let us hike back to my second-grade classroom. Every time we had to think of an idea or produce a project proposal, we went through the "brainstorming process." Being seven years old, it was my least favorite part of the day. We only had ten minutes to come up with a solid idea that could actually be implemented. Since then, I have always hated the idea of brainstorming or producing ideas in a short, limited amount of time. However, when I started coming up with ideas, I eventually realized that I needed to learn to love brainstorming. I learned more about it and understood that you could brainstorm the way you *want* to brainstorm.

I made brainstorming the way I wanted to make it. I realized that creating a doable idea in ten minutes was a real stretch, but I did enjoy the thrill of producing ideas in a limited amount of time. Hence, rather

than making brainstorming a way to get to your final solution, I made it a step that allows you to jot down ANY and EVERY idea you come up with and label them enough to move on to the research phase.

During this step of the innovation process, there is no such thing as a bad idea. In this chapter, we are going to focus on individualized brainstorming, but if you prefer to work with a partner to brainstorm ideas, you are welcome to do so! Teams are a wonderful way to spur ideas and spark innovation. Take that inspiration that you drew from a little bit of research, remind yourself of the current solutions, grab those questions that you answered, and start listing!

Take a second to look around whichever room you are sitting in and set a two-minute timer or watch the clock. I want you to come up with fifteen ideas to make your room better in that amount of time and write them down on a scrap sheet of paper or sticky notes. Right now, do not worry about the problem you already found. Just focus on how you can make your room better! We will get back to that. I know that seems hard, but remember, no idea is a BAD idea. Think of everything possible and do not limit yourself to what you think is "right" or "wrong." Go!

Here is a tip! Remember, *quantity* over *quality*. The number of ideas or topics that you have is much more important than how "good" those ideas are. You will get to narrow your list down in the research step, but try to get as many ideas as possible during this part of the process.

Done? Excellent job! You might be looking down at your list, thinking, "These are not the greatest ideas in the world…." and that is okay! You will have a chance to look through them more in-depth during the research phase.

When I was coming up with Tethys, my lead detection tool, the brainstormed ideas I started out with were well beyond crazy. I had ideas starting from bacteria in the water to eat the lead all the way up to ideas like counteracting lead in water by adding more chemicals in the water. Yes, not the most reasonable solutions in the world. But, if I did not brainstorm any ideas, I would not have had the idea I currently have, which was on my list of ideas.

The more we have, the more we can choose from, and that's exactly what brainstorming helps us do—to get those ideas, to put everything in our head on paper so that we can keep going through the process.

Science Snapshot! Introducing Sofia Ongele. As a student, after finding the issue of gender-based harassment in her local community, Sofia brainstormed and developed an app called "ReDawn" to make sure that nobody else is hurt the same way. It provides victims of harassment a place to gain the support necessary following these traumatic incidents.

Organizing Your Ideas

Now that you or your team have a list of solutions and different ideas, it is time to organize them in a way that can help you move on to the research phase. There are several ways to organize ideas. However, the one that I think is most effective is using a technique called an Affinity Diagram.

An Affinity Diagram allows you to group your ideas into common categories so that it is easier to research in bulk when we move on to the next step. Here is a basic outline of an Affinity Diagram:

Group 1 **Group 2** **Group 3**

Idea		Idea		Idea	

You might have noticed that each of the ideas looks like sticky notes. I like to do my Affinity Diagrams on sticky notes on a wall, digitally, or on a whiteboard. Overall, each sticky note consists of a brainstormed idea that you came up with in a short amount of time. The "Groups" are categories that YOU create to group your ideas successfully. You can have as many Groups and ideas as you like for your solution. For example, here is the Affinity Diagram I developed for Epione:

Treatment **Diagnosis** **Prevention**

Brain stimulation to reduce speed of addiction	Better pain therapy options based on nanomaterials for addiction	Digestible pill to identify addiction in your body	AI Database for early identification of addiction	Game/Webinar to alert people about addiction	Virtual reality warnings and data
Genetic approach towards early treatment		Improved "health survey" at the doctors for more accurate results	Device to diagnose addiction at an early stage using colorimetry	Patch to help with prevention if there is family history	

I now had three clear categories that I wanted to explore in: Treatment, Diagnosis, and Prevention. I then sorted my ten ideas into these three categories. Now, your lengthy list is broken down. But how do you know which one to continue working on?

Here is a tip! For most of the innovation process, your gut feeling is going to make most of the difference. No matter how many tools and mathematical resources you use, the gut feeling and what YOU think personally dominates. Always.

This is simple. Remember that research you did in the beginning? That was not just to list your ideas. It also helps you figure out which category you want to focus on. Try sorting out the gaps in the current solutions you found and even the statistics or biggest area of impact you found into the groups you produced. I found it to be intuitive when I started breaking it down. It felt like everything I thought of magically led to ONE category. The category with the greatest number of gaps, biggest impact, statistics, and ROOT cause of the problem tends to be the one you should focus on the most. If it ends up not being the right one, you can always come back to this point as a "touch-and-go" point.

Coming Up Next

We explored the solution space and narrowed solution ideas down to a manageable set. In the next step, we will dive headlong into researching all the details of the solution, finding and talking to experts in the field, and, finally, narrowing our focus to a single solution we want to develop. We will also talk about other important aspects of product development, such as planning and timeline.

Name: _____

Class: _____ Date: _____

Step 2: Brainstorm Workspace

Please follow along with your teachers as you use this workspace to go through the observing process. Follow the numbers next to each activity/ diagram in chronological order.

1. Initial Research

Jot down the names of the **three sources** you will be performing your research with:

Resource 1: _____

Resource 2: _____

Resource 3: _____

Your Brainstorm Space:

2. Affinity Diagram

After your analysis, what is the category you will focus on researching? Why?

_____

_____

_____

_____

_____

How will you approach your research journey? List some thoughts here:

_____

_____

Don't worry if you're not totally sure yet, we'll discuss this more!

CHAPTER 5

Step 3—Research

I know research is not the most amazing term to hear. I used to shudder just thinking about going through many websites and finding magazines around my house. I could picture my desk cluttered. Yes, a sense of dread is the normal reaction that I get when I tell people research is a crucial step in the innovation process. While it may consist of a lot of websites, days at the library, and other resources, it is much more fun than you think.

I know from personal experience that it is hard to convince people that research can be fun, but the trick for it to be fun is, you must *make* it fun. Through this chapter, I want to share a fun way to do research.

Let us get the elephant out of the room. Why don't most people like to research?

1. It is time-consuming—and you can get stuck with innovator's block.
2. It is boring—there is nothing to spice it up.
3. It is hard to do—like how many books and websites can a human sort through? It is sometimes super complex. There is also the challenge of developing a reading skill, especially as you work toward more academic language heavy work.

All of this is true, and the first step to getting rid of those issues is to accept that it is an issue. Let us start out by understanding what the purpose of research is.

By performing research, we can come up with an idea that is solid, feasible, and doable. Even though research might be the hardest step, it is the step that takes you the furthest, and that is amazing during the innovation process.

Science Snapshot! Meet Maya Lee. As a high school freshman, she started a foundation, Team UKAPS, or Uniting Kids Against Poverty and Sickness. Amidst the COVID-19 pandemic, the foundation united kids worldwide to organize food drives for their community food pantries and purchase meals from local restaurants, delivering them to heroic health care workers. Team UKAPS's goal is to help dozens of more communities, even after the COVID-19 pandemic.

Finding Mentors and Experts

Before you start, you might have more in-depth questions that you have been researching but would love to have even more information about. This is your cue to reach out to a variety of people to find a mentor or an expert that you can depend on for research. As a student, we are limited with the knowledge we have or are introduced to at school or other places. We can search the internet, read books, and read articles. However, some of the research articles are at a level that we need experts or professors to decode them for us or explain them to us in simple words.

It is great to have a mentor's perspective and the second set of eyes confirming what you are working on, giving them the opportunity to help you find alternatives when you hit a setback or introducing you to more tools that you can use! Sometimes it is just a confirmation of support and motivation when you need it in the process!

But how do you know who to look for as an expert? Aha! Great question! It is a simple process, but it can be frustrating at times:

- · Look for local communities, lab managers, and professors in the area of your research and make a list of what you are looking for from each one of them.
- · Create a video with your idea and draft an email or plan out a phone call requesting exactly what you are looking for and send it to the people you shortlisted.
- · DO NOT worry about asking to be mentored. It is not dumb at all! (I was so frustrated about the first couple of emails I sent since I kept getting a repetitive no, but soon enough, I realized that "NO" was the worst answer I was going to get...and that's nothing to be afraid of.)
- · Follow-up every week and be organized as to who you followed up with (I got an 80 percent negative response and a 20 percent positive response or further pointers, and that made all the difference).
- · If somebody is open to mentoring you, ask what they will expect from you, then meet or exceed the expectation. Ensure you are on the right track by communicating every single thought with them.

I did a little bit of digging, and I found one of my original emails to an expert I reached out to and received a positive response from! I transferred it into a basic sample format:

Hello {INSERT NAME OF EXPERT},

Introduce yourself: (*My name is Gitanjali Rao. I am an eleven-year-old and sixth grader at Brentwood Middle School in Tennessee.*) Your request: (*I am drafting this email, hoping that you can help me with a significant project I am currently working on.*)

What is your project? (*My project is a proposal to develop a tool that helps with speedy detection of lead contamination in water using a fast, reliable, and inexpensive method. The idea is to detect changes in resistance level—due to the presence of lead—with specially designed carbon nanotube arrays. Concisely, I am proposing using the change in electrical conductivity of carbon nanotube arrays to detect lead and its compounds. This technique has been used for the detection of gases in your toxic gas detector, but not for compounds such as lead compounds in liquids.*)

Short Video: (*Attached is a short video to learn more!*)

Expanded Request and Timeline: (*Since you specialize in interesting projects using nanotube and nanotechnology, I have three requests for you, by July 28th if possible:*)

Clear Action Items:
- (*I wanted to seek your opinion on my proposed solution and its feasibility in the real world. I would love to receive any corrections or suggestions.*
- *Given that your subject area is fascinating to me, I was wondering if there was any research that is currently going on about nanomaterials related to this subject? I would appreciate it if you could point me to any other current research or resources.*
- *I am particularly interested in any way you can help me understand the process of how carbon nanotube arrays can be "seeded/embedded" with lead affinity atoms. I will be glad to work with anybody you can recommend.*)

Express Gratitude: (*Hoping for your positive response, and any help would be greatly appreciated.*)

Thanks, and warm regards,

{INSERT YOUR NAME}

Here is a tip! Make sure to spend a good chunk of your time discussing your project or idea. Also, state a CLEAR deadline and set of action items to give your expert an easy method to contact you and provide you everything you need! The longer the email, the less likely professors/researchers will take the time to engage with it.

Once I sent out this email, I followed up with more questions and phone calls to help emphasize the idea that I WAS interested, and I did want to continue pursuing my idea.

Remember, it can be frustrating because you might get quite a few nos. But keep trying to reach your goal, because one person made all the difference for me. Tell yourself that if you find your one person, you will have an easy resource to get more details. Tell yourself that you will be more productive with an expert to guide you. Let us head on back to that tool I told you about.

For research to be fun, we must *make* it fun. I want to share a method that can get rid of those earlier problems we saw and help you have fun while doing it.

Identifying a Solution

Let us start with the design criteria. By now, you know the gaps in the current solutions for the problem you picked to solve.

You might have found at least one gap in the current solution. The more, the better!

Now define how your solution should look:

- What is the main gap the solution should address?
- Should it solve all the gaps in the current solution?
- Should it be affordable? How affordable, based on current solutions?
- Should it be portable?
- Who should and will use it?
- How user-friendly can you make it?

Here is a tip! Try to connect everything you are deciding on your design criteria BACK to your current solutions and your impact. Everything needs to relate to the final goal, which is the impact you will be making with it.

If you do not like to write, sketch the solution, and label it. Here are examples of some sketches my team created when we were seven years old. The picture does not have to be perfect, and you need not be an artist. The picture should simply bring out what you are thinking about.

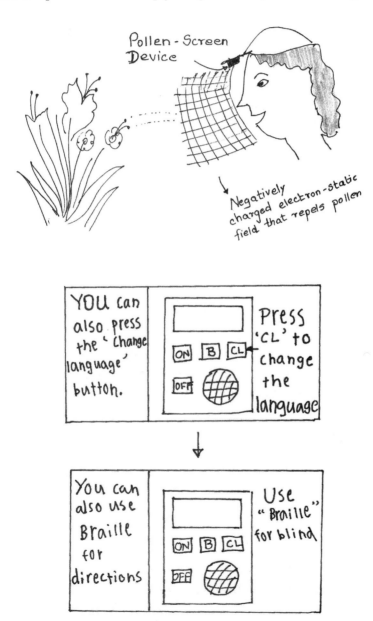

Pollen - Screen Device

Negatively charged electron-static field that repels pollen

YOU can also press the 'Change language' button.

Press 'CL' to change the language

You can also use Braille for directions

Use "Braille" for blind

Now that you have an idea, find out what technologies may fit your solution. Try to come up with at least two solutions to every problem you found or to the causes of each problem. To come up with a solution initially, you can just mention something at a very high level, such as "A device that helps find a black-box underwater faster" or "An enhanced black-box that sends out signals to the airport of where it is located." You really do not have to define whether you are going to use satellite communication technology or GPS or 3D printed devices, etc. Just keep it at a basic level to not overwhelm yourself. If you know what to use, add it as a note.

Next up, introducing matrices! When I was explaining this concept to my friends, a lot of the responses I got were:

"Oh! It's that thing that we do in Calculus!"

"Is this what my mom does when she says she works in Information Technology?"

"I know EXACTLY what this is. It's that thing I learned in geology class the other day!"

Okay, well, *technically*, their point of view could be considered right. But the type of matrices we are going to be working on today is entirely different.

If there is one thing that you should know about me, it is that I love competition. I love watching a competition, I love being part of a competition, and I like creating competition (in the healthiest way possible) because it gives me horsepower to keep moving ahead. When we are working with matrices, we are setting up a competition between the different ideas that we brainstormed.

If you have watched the Olympics, I am sure you are aware of the gymnastics event. If you have not, each of the contestants lines up to do a series of events such as beams, floor, etc.

There is a panel of judges that judge their ability to create their version of a "perfect routine." They judge them on a variety of different skills, some of which include:

- How difficult is the routine they performed?
- How well was the routine executed?
- Were there any penalties during the execution?

The judges take some of these factors more seriously than others. For example, the judges might take the execution of the routine more seriously than the difficulty or penalties, meaning that it is "weighted" more. Based on this, the judges can decide a winner for the specific event.

My point is, this is exactly how you are going to judge your ideas—like an Olympic gymnastics event! Here is an example of a matrix:

Category/Weighting	Idea 1	TOTAL	Idea 2	TOTAL	Idea 3	TOTAL	Idea 4	TOTAL
Impact (5)		5 x _		5 x _		5 x _		5 x _
Feasibility (4)		4 x _		4 x _		4 x _		4 x _
Cost (3)		3 x _		3 x _		3 x _		3 x _
Portability (2)		2 x _		2 x _		2 x _		2 x _
Ease of Use (1)		1 x _		1 x _		1 x _		1 x _
MEGA TOTAL	XXXX		XXXX		XXXX		XXXX	

To explain a little bit about what is going on here, on the left-most column that says "Category/Weighting," those are the five distinct categories that I have set up based on *my* judgment. The weightings help me understand what is most important in my eyes. I think impact is most important, so I set that as the highest weighting. I think ease of use is least important, so I set that as the lowest weighting.

Each of the columns that contain different idea numbers gives you the chance to rate each of your "contestants" (ideas) in that category. Each of the columns that say "TOTAL" allows you to multiply your rating to your weight. It is okay if you do not get it right now, you will understand what I mean from my completed matrix for Epione later in this chapter.

The bottom-most row titled "MEGA TOTAL" gives you the chance to add up your "TOTAL" values to get your final winner!

Here is an example of my matrix for Epione:

First, here is my idea list so that you can refer to it:

- *Idea 1—Digestible pill to identify addiction in your body*
- *Idea 2—Device to diagnose addiction at an early stage using colorimetry*

- *Idea 3—Improved "health survey" at the doctors for more accurate results*
- *Idea 4—Game/Webinar to alert people about addiction*

Category/Weighting	Idea 1	TOTAL	Idea 2	TOTAL	Idea 3	TOTAL	Idea 4	TOTAL
Impact (5)	4	20 _	5	25	2	10 _	1	5 _
Feasibility (4)	2	8 _	4	16	3	12 _	3	12 _
Cost (3)	1	3 _	3	9	5	15 _	4	12 _
Portability (2)	5	10 _	4	8	5	10 _	3	6 _
Ease of Use (1)	4	4 _	4	4	5	5 _	4	4 _
MEGA TOTAL	XXXX	45	XXXX	63	XXXX	52	XXXX	39

Here, I used the same four categories as the empty matrix I showed you earlier. I ranked each of my ideas on a scale from one to five, with five being really good and one being not the best. For example, the cost of Idea 1 was not really the best, but the cost of Idea 3 was awesome! I determined these by doing a little bit of research about each topic and understanding more about it. Then, using my "formula," I multiplied my *ranking* with the *weighting* determined and put that in the total column. For example, I rated the impact of Idea 1 as a four, and my weighting for impact was a five, so I multiplied four x five to get my final total, which was twenty. Once I used my formula for ALL the ideas and ALL the columns, I added up the TOTAL values and put them in the MEGA TOTAL row. I then highlighted the idea with the highest score and crowned it the "winner."

Here is a tip! If you are still struggling to understand the process of matrices (especially because it is hard to describe it in a book), check out my YouTube channel "Just STEM Stuff" and the video titled "How to Narrow Down Your Ideas" to understand the concept further.

Congratulations! If you fill that out, you have AN idea that you have filed down from a lengthy list of ideas and, hopefully, it was not boring, it was not super time-consuming, and it was fun! *You* made researching fun!

Creating a Timeline

Alright, one last step before we can move on. Creating a timeline! Surely, you might have an idea, but you also have this tiny spur of fear in your mind telling you, "There's NO way I can build all of this." What if I told you you did not have to build ALL OF IT. "But…but…that defeats the whole purpose of this book." Not at ALL! Even though you have an idea, spread it out, break it up. Come back to this book when you are ready to move on. What I am saying is, create a timeline. Timelines are a way for you to keep yourself on track and set deadlines for yourself. I like to draw out timelines, so I know what I am going to get done next week, the week after, a month after, even a year! Currently, for Epione, I have a timeline running until the end of 2022.

Here is a tip! Do not stress too much about how far you want your timeline to go! My first few timelines only reached out a couple of months. If you DO have a multiple-year plan, go ahead and put that into place. However, if you just want to focus on working for maybe a few days or weeks, feel free to put that into a timeline as well!

Here is a digital model of Epione's timeline. Notice that the plans are beyond a prototype. I am not sure whether I can achieve this exactly, but I go after it.

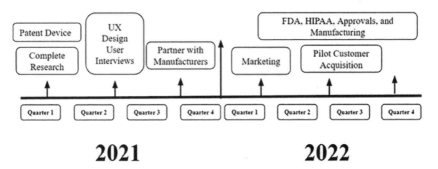

This is a good time to reflect on your journey so far and start making future plans so that you know what to expect as you go through the rest of the innovation process.

Coming Up Next

We have narrowed our solution, and we have done enough research to know the solution approach well. In the next chapter, Step 3, we will get right down to building our solution. We will talk about tools and technology options to consider and keep in our toolbox. We will try to figure out the best approach to develop a working product using a combination of technologies available to us today.

Name: _____

Class: _____ Date: _____

Step 3: Researching Workspace

Please follow along with your teachers as you use this workspace to go through the observing process. Follow the numbers next to each activity/ diagram in chronological order.

1. Research Approach

- Books/Handheld Resources
- Online Papers & Web Browsing
- Videos & Multimedia Resources
- Speaking with Experts/Communication
- Hands-On Activities
- Other: _____

Write down everything you know about your topic here without doing any research:

2. Mentorship Requests

Draft out an email to a mentor or expert that you would like to work with:

_____

_____

_____

_____

_____

_____

_____

_____

3. Matrix Fill-Up

Category/Weighting	Idea 1	TOTAL	Idea 2	TOTAL	Idea 3	TOTAL	Idea 4	TOTAL
Impact (5)		5 x _		5 x _		5 x _		5 x _
Feasibility (4)		4 x _		4 x _		4 x _		4 x _
Cost (3)		3 x _		3 x _		3 x _		3 x _
Portability (2)		2 x _		2 x _		2 x _		2 x _
Ease of Use (1)		1 x _		1 x _		1 x _		1 x _
MEGA TOTAL	XXXX		XXXX		XXXX		XXXX	

What is your final solution? What steps have you taken so far to find it?

_____

_____

_____

_____

_____

_____

_____

4. Project Timeline

| Quarter 1 | Quarter 2 | Quarter 3 | Quarter 4 | Quarter 1 | Quarter 2 | Quarter 3 | Quarter 4 |

CHAPTER 6

Step 4—Building

Woohoo! We have made it to my personal favorite step, Building. The reason that I really enjoy building is that it is super hands-on. Yes, the other activities are interactive, but as a kinesthetic learner, I cannot wait to build and use my hands to do something cool! You can start building smaller pieces of your solution as you are researching. You can sketch as many times as you want and define what you need to build your solution.

Traditional Problem-Solving vs. Design Thinking

For a long time, we have relied on a time-tested traditional method of problem-solving that takes a specific approach to breaking down a problem and solving it. However, there is another approach that forms the backbone of my process, especially the "Observe" and "Build" steps, and it is formally called "Design Thinking." Before I go on to other topics, I wanted to spend some time here highlighting the difference in the approaches.

Let us try to understand both approaches and learn why a Design Thinking-based approach is better and is increasingly popular.

Traditional Approach: A traditional approach is the most common, default way of how we solve a problem. We take a problem, gather all the information we can about the problem, and then go about solving it by assessing the feasibility of the solution, etc. This is straightforward, linear, and structured.

Here is an example. Let us say the customers of a home security system are complaining that their devices are often raising false alarms.

A standard linear approach to solving this problem is straightforward:

- **Step 1**—Identify the problem: From all the feedback the company received, it is well-established that the problem was the devices were generating false alarms.
- **Step 2**—Gather all available information about the problem: The customers' complaints and the validation from the service center agents provide the firm with all the details needed, such as the device model and absence of incidents that the system was designed for, such as break-ins, fire, etc.
- **Step 3**—Narrow the solution options: The firm then produces a hypothesis of three reasons, ranging from poor sensors to poor configuration and user error, where the customer has placed the device in a non-recommended location. They narrow it down to fine-tuning of the sensor to identify the same problem as before, such as motion and smoke detection.
- **Step 4**—Develop the solution that is most feasible and hope the problem is fixed: The firm fixes the software in the sensor and updates the software on all the devices with their customers and future products.

So, what do you think of this approach?

While it might solve the problem for some of the customers, the process still leaves quite a few gaping holes that tell us that the solution did not fix the problem. For example, what if the false alarms were not false alarms? What if the sensors thought that there was a human being in the room, but it turns out it was a pet? What if it truly was something a customer did, like placing the sensor in a non-ideal location? What if the customer filed a complaint about a false alarm but never really considered that the motion sensor was switched on?

All these questions and the corresponding information can only be discovered if the problem is looked at from a customer point of view. Similarly, the solution the firm devised, while optimal and feasible from their perspective, might not be ideal for the customer. If the problem never was about sensor sensitivity, then the customer's problem never went away. There are many such reasons why traditional techniques for problem-solving fall short. We need an alternative process that addresses these gaps.

Design Thinking: Now that we understand the traditional approach, let us look at the Design Thinking approach. Broadly, Design Thinking is less linear and less structured than a traditional approach. While it is like a traditional approach in some ways as it also breaks down the problem and considers the data, it does not, however, assume that everything we need to solve the problem is completely based on the data provided. It uses the general idea of the problem and the data in hand to look at the problem from the consumer's perspective. Sometimes the real problem is never highlighted. The whole premise is to empathize with the customer and come up with a list of both declared and undeclared sets of problems that are causes of concern for the customer. This information is then used to solve the problem in a unique way.

Let us look at our example and try solving the problem using a Design Thinking approach. First, let us understand the core principles of Design Thinking:

Empathy with a User: A large part of the Design Thinking process is to look at the problem from the end-user perspective. Users are not always clear about explaining the problem and providing all the data relevant to the context of the problem. Either nobody asks them explicitly, or sometimes, users themselves are shy about saying some things that sound too obvious. It is the job of the folks who are solving the problem to imagine and explore all avenues and scenarios, in addition to the ones provided, so that there is a collection of a broad set of reasons. Similarly, when it comes to developing solutions, it is a lot more valuable to seek feedback from the end-users and narrow optimal solutions that best address the needs of the actual user.

Divergent and Convergent Design: Unlike traditional thinking, where the process is to narrow both the problem and viable solutions before addressing the issue, Design Thinking deliberately expands on problem space and possible solution options in the solution space before settling on a possible solution. The goal is not to get bogged down by constraints and to instead imagine all options before reaching the tentative solution. Tentative because we are not done yet.

Prototyping: A possible solution is then developed quickly into a prototype to not only validate the design but also to seek user feedback.

Test, Fail, Iterate Cycle: Unlike a traditional linear process, design thinking is in a constant loop of building, testing, failing, and iterating, with the customer at the center of it all.

Overall, the flow of a Design Thinking-based solution development looks as follows.

The concept of Design Thinking emphasizes the need to put oneself in the end user's shoes, constantly iterate with prototypes, and always accept that things will need to change to build a superior solution that truly addresses the needs. In our cases, we can further expand our problem space beyond whatever the end-user states by getting creative and looking at our scenarios. Once the problem space is defined, we get to a solution phase where we again expand the possible solution space by adding a solution that might not even be workable. Our goal currently is not to worry about constraints but to keep thinking about expanding the possible options, assuming there were no constraints. We then transition to developing solutions, which is nothing but a bunch of prototypes that are waiting for user feedback. Once we get through the deliberate cycle of build and iterate, exploring all possible options, we can then settle on a single solution we now know with fair certainty would be comprehensive. In our case, a solution turns out to be a new sensor capability that needed to be added to the device that separates humans from pets when detecting motion.

As we will see in the coming section, as we get more into building solutions, my process adopts the Design Thinking principles and expands on it with some practical additions to work within the bounds of limited cost and time a teenager has for their projects.

Developing a Prototype

What is our goal with building? Building is a broad term, and it is important for us to understand what we want to end up with. The thing with building is that this is the step that differentiates the innovation process from the scientific process. Overall, we do not necessarily have to worry about coming up with the most beautiful product in the world. Our goal at this step is to come up with a rough sketch or design of what we want to build.

The media that you can use to "build" are:

- Paper
- Online software
- Physical model
- And many other tools!

Here is a tip! When you are sketching out an idea, do it fast, and do it messy. You want to spend more time coming up with an idea rather than perfecting your drawings. If you can understand it, you are in a perfect place.

The choice is yours. How you want to demonstrate your idea is *your* choice. Before we hop into expanding your original idea, I want to focus on building a physical product.

As a reminder, this physical product does not have to be amazing, and it does not have to be ready to sell. This is a *prototype*, and even if your first idea does not look exactly the way you want it to look, it is OKAY! That is what the iteration process is for, which we will get into later in this book. I want to break up building a prototype into three parts:

1. Finding materials
2. Now what?
3. Putting something together

Finding materials to build something seems like a challenging task. Maybe you cannot go to the store right this second, or you do not have a full science lab in your room—that is OKAY! Materials do not have to be the fanciest 3-D printer or laser cutter that you can find out there. Let us do a fun exercise.

- *You have two minutes to go to another room in your house and pick out four objects that each cost less than seventy-five cents. Some examples are a paperclip, a sheet of paper, a pencil, a thumbtack—just to name a few. Now go!*

Do you have your objects? Awesome. Before we do anything with them, let us talk a bit about the lingering question of "Now what?" That is something that seems to come up a lot. Now that I have everything I need to start building, how am I supposed to throw this together with a couple of scrap parts? How do I plan this out? Right?

I have an answer for you, and it is one you might not like. Try NOT planning. As someone who likes thorough instructions, sometimes "NOT" planning frustrates me, but going with the flow always seems to work better. Let us keep going with the exercise.

- *Spend about ten minutes putting these objects together to build something cool. It can solve a problem; it can just be something cool to look at—it can even be a toy.*

Now that you have your "creation," try reflecting on it. How did that rush of energy feel? If you are someone who likes planning things out, was that frustrating? If it was, how do you plan to get around that feeling next time? If you are a parent or a teacher, how do you guide at this point? How do you help someone who is frustrated reinvest/re-engage?

However, within the building process, there is also a layer of iteration. Iteration is the process of refining your idea continuously so that you end up with the best and most effective idea. Something you create might have to be re-created because it is not big enough for your needs, or it does not completely solve it. Back to our exercise:

- *Take that creation that you have built and demolish it. It is hard to say goodbye, but sometimes it is what is necessary. Now, those scrap parts are gold. Try building it into something different. Again, anything you want!*

Whether you realized it or not, you just successfully completed the exercise and now have two cool builds that you can apply somewhere else in your innovation journey.

Here is my first draft of my anti-cyber-bullying app, Kindly. Since it is an app, it is a little bit different. But I built my first prototype using MIT App Inventor 2, and I did it in less than ten minutes just so that I had an idea of what I wanted the application to look like.

Let us look at my lead-detection device, Tethys. Here is my first prototype of Tethys before I got it to the point where it is currently. The first one took about fifteen minutes to create. It was made from cardboard, and I believe it was originally a Bluetooth speaker box. I looked around my house and dug through my recycling bin to find stuff that I did not use.

Defining Features

Sweet! You are at the point where you have a prototype or at least an idea for a prototype. At this point, I like to define the design criteria, features, and functionalities of this prototype. Maybe you thought about this during your research process, but it gives you more of an opportunity to dive in and understand what your idea really does.

Here is a tip! You worked on defining your design criteria in the research process by figuring out what topics to start putting down in your matrices. Feel free to use those and use the tips below to expand on your design criteria!

Here is an example of basic design criteria:

- Easy to use
- Accurate
- Faster
- Cheaper
- Portable

Prioritize it in the order of importance to the users. Chances are the first two criteria you came up with is your innovation and the solution's core functionality. The rest may be just for convenience to the user. This will remind you of what you want to focus on when you are building.

Features are what is unique about your idea, what components it includes. Let us take a water slide for an example. Some common features of a water slide are:

- Slick slide
- Non-slip stairs
- Safety rail
- Water heater
- Heavy-grip landing pad

They might not make much sense at first, but they provide a basic understanding of what makes the slide better and more unique than other water slides.

Secondly, we look at the functionalities. The functionalities are how various features work and what their purposes are. Essentially, the features are the *what,* and the functionalities are the *why and how.*

Some functionalities of the features of the water slide are:

- Slick slide—Latest in plastic, for smooth and fast action for the rider
- Non-slip stairs—Stainless-steel coating, to ensure a safe entrance to the slide
- Safety rail—Metal rail within sides of the slide, to slow down or speed up the slide for maximum engagement
- Water heater—Embedded within the water feature, for a comfortable ride
- Heavy-grip landing pad—Pronged rubber, for a fast but safe landing

So, I encourage you to start thinking about the features and functionalities of the idea you researched. In the meantime, here is one of my feature and functionalities charts for the home screen of Kindly. Keep in mind this one is a little bit different because it is an app, but it uses the SAME basic rules:

Something you probably noticed here was I included a sketch or an early prototype of the home screen of Kindly. This is a fantastic way to break down an idea and put your prototype on paper.

Science Snapshot! Tate Schrock is a student from rural Colorado hoping to make a difference in his community. Growing up on his family's farm, Tate found that soil sampling was an arduous process, especially for many acres of farmland. Hence, Tate built, coded, and productized an on-land, soil-probe rover to be able to make the sampling process much faster and efficient.

Emerging Technologies

We are living in interesting times where newer technologies are not only shaping our future but also offering opportunities for innovation. Technology is what we can build with, and we should continue to look at the world around us and build upwards from there. Sometimes I think, "There's nothing left to invent or innovate." Well, obviously there is because you came up with several problems to solve. There have been some awesome discoveries, but let us look at other technology we can build from.

5G Wireless

Let us take wireless technology and the standard that defines bandwidth and speed of communication. Wireless technology is not only important for our phones and handhelds; it has the potential to eliminate the need for hard-wired physical cable connections. In other words, instead of fiber optic cables running to our homes and businesses, in the future—with increased bandwidths and network speeds—all communications can be over wireless technology. 4G, the current standard, while a vast improvement over earlier generals of network technology, is still a bit slow for any real-time interactions that require almost negligible lag. 5G wireless technology, a successor to 4G, is already here. A 20G/sec 5G speed offers near real-time interaction with almost no lag. Instantaneous communication with near-zero lag might sound like faster internet and better video, but it also has a profound impact on everything we cannot do well today.

What about the opportunity for remote surgery? This is a significant capability where nobody needs to die because a surgeon cannot make it to the surgery room in person. Any expert surgeon anywhere in the world could operate remotely. However, the problem with today's speeds is that there is a small but noticeable lag between a surgeon's move and the resulting action on the patient. Even a split-second lag can have dire consequences for critical surgeries where the remote surgeon must react almost instantaneously.

With 5G speeds, it is expected that there will be close to zero lag, thus making instantaneous communication a reality. Similarly, instead of people having to be physically present in meetings or isolated in video conferencing, hologram presence can be a reality. Imagine the possibilities when nobody is present in a room, but everybody is sitting next to each other?

In addition, novel devices and technologies could become very portable and could send many more points of data for effective analysis.

Nanotechnology

Nanotechnology has made huge strides in the past decade and is something that is going to be the core of a lot of new innovations in this century. Technically, nanotechnology is a fabrication and modification of certain specific elements at atomic and molecular levels. Nanotechnology created materials, products, and limitless opportunities for us to exploit micro-level particles called nanoparticles. Whole fields of medicines, material sciences, chemistry, etc. are re-evaluating and altering traditional approaches to solutions because nanotechnology-based derivatives are now offering cheaper, more reliable, and robust solution alternatives.

Nanomaterials come in many shapes, such as spiral, tubular, and so on. Carbon nanostructures such as flat-surface graphene and ball-like fullerene have already garnered Nobel recognition for its inventors due to the enormous impact it has had on our lives. Others structure like cylindrical-shaped carbon nanotubes, cone-shaped carbon nano-cones, and carbon nanohorns are showing increasing promise in various applications due to a combination of their unique shapes and their combinations with other elements. Carbon nanotubes themselves can create multiple options to experiment with their shapes that range from single-walled and multi-walled to the way the atoms are oriented in the tube, such as the armchair, chiral, etc. Each combination provides a unique set of interesting properties that can be used to solve specific problems. Additionally, when combined with other elements, also called dopants, such as nitrogen, boron, even hydrogen, give nanotubes unique capabilities such as enhanced electrical properties that can be used to develop sensors and other solutions not possible before. Carbon nanostructures function in a unique way because they take the already excellent electrical conductivity properties of carbon and amplify them when configured in a special shape. This increased electrical property provides opportunities for many applications that were not conceivable before due to prohibitive costs and difficulty in construction.

Doping is an added specialized technique where atoms from specific elements are used to replace some of the carbon atoms in a nanostructure, which changes the electrical properties of a nanotube, allowing it to develop solutions by measuring variations in properties on the nanostructure. Nanotechnology also allows the development of bots, some smaller than viruses, which can target specific cells and cure diseases. Nanobots, the size of viruses, can be effectively deployed to treat many ailments ranging from cancer to viral infections. Maybe there is a cure for future pandemics waiting in nanotechnology?

Power of Data and Analytics

People are generating 2.5 quintillion bytes of data each day. Nearly 90 percent of all data has been created in the last two years. We are living in a world today where we are surrounded by data. Data we generate, data machines generate, data that is collected, and data that is analyzed. Analytics or analysis of data to create some insight is, today, providing us an opportunity to ask questions and explore scenarios that we did not think was possible just a few years back. The mining of years of data gives us not only trends and a report of the state of things but also insights that we did not know existed. Historical medical records can show not only how trends of various cancer treatments have evolved and their effectiveness but can also unearth new diagnostics relationships. Sophisticated data science algorithms can take historical data and project or predict how things will evolve in the future, providing an unprecedented opportunity in shaping public policy, social infrastructure, healthcare, and community development, not to mention scientific innovation.

The next evolution of this trend, which we will talk about shortly, is the development of machines and artificial intelligence that can "learn" from historical data and trends to mimic future behavior.

There are enough tools and technologies today—especially on cloud-based technology providers that have made gathering and operating on data easier—that the barrier to learning has been lowered, and value from data and analytics has been derived.

Artificial Intelligence

The last century was about machines performing repetitive tasks, but artificial intelligence (AI) now allows machines to also think and decide like humans. Imagine, everyday decisions that currently require human capacity and experience to decide the best options will soon be replaced by intelligence that learns from our collective history and provides the best recommendations. We talked about the opportunity with data, specifically mining of data for insights and trends. AI builds on this core to adopt learning algorithms that can estimate a probability for something happening and take suitable action. The intelligence part comes in when the consequence of this action, good or bad, is fed back into the system for future decision making. Imagine an AI that can recommend a restaurant based on your preferences. If the best recommendation the machine gives is not what you need, the feedback you provide pipes back into the AI engine. Next time it will remember your preference. This is how AI learns, and AI's increased intelligence is a huge lift in easing how we work and make decisions. The idea of "Internet of Things" was floated a few years back to describe a new technological concept where everything we use in our daily life is now technologically enabled to communicate and exchanges information. We've all heard of autonomous vehicles, but with the advent of the age of "Internet of Things," the combination of data analytics, artificial intelligence, and high-speed networks, technology will soon enable vehicles, tools, devices that will to talk to everything else, on ultra-fast networks, and making intelligent decisions that benefit the broader community.

Virtual and Augmented Reality

Imagine a world where we can go places without ever leaving our chairs. These places can be as vast as the depths of the Grand Canyon or as infinitesimal as the tiny circuits of a laptop circuit board. Imagine the possibilities of building, trying out, and simulating components in a virtual world before spending time and energy on building a physical solution. Virtual reality offers such a possibility. It is a world created digitally to simulate the real-world and its attributes. With advances in processing speeds, graphics, and visualization tools, virtual reality has started to move from science fiction to practical reality. What used to be more common in the gaming world is increasingly getting transferred to real applications. Doctors can learn better techniques to operate safely, explore diseases that are difficult to understand, and identify problems in the internals of the human body. Mechanics and technicians can now better service machinery assisted by details and notes augmenting what they see. People can meet and collaborate globally, all using virtual reality. It is cheaper in the long run, provides more opportunities to try out things that we could not in the real world, is more environmentally friendly, and, most importantly, helps solve problems in ways that we could not even imagine before.

Augmented reality (or AR) is a flavor of virtual reality, where the real world is supplemented or augmented with virtual reality. Imagine a camera with augmented reality features. When we look through the camera view in a city square, normally we would see all the things around us, like shops or cafés and streets. However, let us say we want to know the names of the streets or the kinds of things the shops are selling. With AR turned on, the camera will not only show the real world around, but overlap the streets with digital street names, show us short descriptions of the shops along with what they sell and how good their ratings are, or direct us to the nearest place to get pizza. This is a powerful tool when we consider the implications of this technology and the opportunities it provides. Now factories can equip their workers with AR glasses so that they know exactly which part to fix and how to fix it. No more costly errors or long training programs. Similarly, surgeons with AR glasses can get an accurate, possibly real-time picture of the patient and their anatomy to complete an operation safely and successfully.

Genetics/Genetic Engineering

Since the discoveries of Gregor Mendel, the founder of the modern science of genetics, the role of genetics in determining traits in living organisms has been well-established. However, research in genetics and genetic engineering has taken off in the last twenty years due to the mapping of genomes (or genetic code) of organisms (including humans) and to the cutting-edge techniques of manipulating genetic code at cellular levels.

Traditional diagnostic and treatment procedures have evolved in the last few hundred years to identify symptoms and treat the underlying ailment. However, this has not always been highly effective for diagnosis when patients cannot self-diagnose symptoms or if an ailment is genetically inherited. Similarly, not all diseases and ailments can be treated, and any treatment administered is temporary at best. Gene-based techniques such as genetic engineering, computational genomics, and genome mapping allow the diagnosis of conditions at the most basic level and provide the ability to consider opportunities for a cure. Home mini-PCR kits and CRISPR gene-editing techniques using Cas9/Cas12a enzymes are the latest path-breaking developments allowing a broader interest in the technology. Interestingly, gene-based identification of ancestry and health conditions has become a successful business model. We are just starting to scratch the surface of the possibilities of building new products, solutions, treatments, and diagnostic procedures using a more fundamental building block of the body, the genes. There are many labs and universities that are doing excellent work in the field that share their research often.

Tools and Techniques

Perhaps you have iterated through the ideation process countless times, and you want to now get on with building something real. Before we jump right into it, let us take a second to go over some technical tools and useful skills that you can use to build and develop your ideas even further. Here is a note: if you do not understand these concepts on your first go, that is okay! This is just here for reference, in case you would like to work more with these technologies in the future. There is a lot of material, guides, and reference documentation online that you can refer to for more in-depth details.

Microcontrollers and Microcomputers

A lot of initiatives and solutions require the use of automation, sensors, electrical functions, and signals. You can try creating mechanical solutions such as motors, solar cells, physical, electronic circuits with components soldered on breadboards, or printed circuit boards, etc. Up until a few years ago, this was the norm, and every project required ground-up work on developing components. Despite spending a lot of time putting things together instead of focusing on novel ways to improve a particular device or new piece of technology, it would still end up as an inflexible solution, prone to breakdowns and repairs.

In the last few years, technology has changed. We are now in the age of small, portable, inexpensive, programmable devices that can be configured to address a variety of needs such as sensing, logic-based control of components, complex simultaneous operations, etc. These give us not only the flexibility of design but also allow us to fail safely and produce innovative ideas to develop better solutions. These have inbuilt support for multiple display types, various pluggable sensors, Bluetooth-based or Wi-Fi wireless communication, and are all program-mable so that we do not have to mess around with hard-wired electronic solutions that are difficult to change.

These products generally fall in the category called microcontrollers and microcomputers. The most common ones are Adafruit, Arduino, and Raspberry Pi. The following table explains general differences and what I believe you should use them for. Of course, you can get creative and use them for many other things! There is a great table for reference on the opposite page.

Attribute	Adafruit	Arduino	Raspberry Pi
What It Is	A popular, small size micro-controller with features to manage the flow of information and inbuilt ports for sensors	Another popular single-board microcontroller. Compatible with Adafruit and has a bit more features than Adafruit for some models	A micropro-cessor with capabilities for hosting a Linux OS running multiple execu-tion threads. Comes inte-grated with support for ethernet, video, and audio.
When to Use It	For operations that require control of flows, execution of a single function, low-energy Bluetooth, Wi-Fi communications	Low power needs with control of flow such as simple repetitive tasks, lower level hardware access, execution of a single function, low-energy Bluetooth, Wi-Fi communications	Full micropro-cessing needs; capabilities such as multi-function execution, inte-grated support for hardware, high power utility needs, large storage needs
When Not to Use	Multiple func-tions need to run simultane-ously, things that require more processing power, web applications, and controls	Need for complex processing needs such as image processing, real-time network communications, storage of data, in-memory processing	When space is at a premium, and there is not a need for multi-processing capabilities. No use for inte-grated hardware or large memory or operating system

For example, if you are trying to build a device that has a temperature sensor, and you want to read the temperature at different intervals, do something with the temperature values, and display it. You can use a controller like Adafruit and Arduino very effectively. If you want to do other things in the same project, such as take pictures and process images, store data, and create reports, then a higher computing solution like Raspberry Pi would be best.

But do not necessarily limit your idea or solution to just one microcontroller or computer. You can use a variety of different microcontrollers and combine them together to complete different functionalities. You can also experiment with a variety of different controllers and see what gets your job done the best. A lot of what you do with microcontrollers is experimentation.

Another big part of microcontrollers and computers is the coding aspect. You can refer to the chart above to look at the language you program in for each of the different controllers. Coding sounds scary when you start to get into it, but by doing some reading and using guides for your controllers, you can find great resources to start going with the basics. I put in some great starter websites to look at in the "Resources" section of this book.

Wireless Communication

Next up, a lot of projects have portability as a requirement. This means we should be able to easily carry a tool/product/solution and use it. This means that we not only have to communicate wirelessly but also have a power source—like a battery—that lasts longer. While Wi-Fi works great in regular usage, it is not the best option for devices that are supposed to be portable and have limited power capacity. Bluetooth technology is the best out there for communication, as most devices today support the protocol. However, wireless communication over regular Bluetooth can be battery intensive. Hence, consider lightweight protocols such as Bluetooth Low Energy (or BLE). BLE, luckily, is supported by most providers. You have to learn to program BLE differently, but it can be a great alternative for fast, lightweight wireless communication.

These portability solutions can be EASILY embedded within some of your microcontroller work. You can attach external Bluetooth or use the

Adafruit processor with the inbuilt BLE to create devices or solutions that are able to connect to other external devices.

Mobile Applications

For a solution to be effective and usable, it is not enough for it to just be functional. It needs a great user interface that a user is familiar with and that is easy to use and accessible. Mobile applications, hence, are oftentimes a perfect solution. People using mobile phones are already used to that interface and experience.

It is also important to note here that while we are talking about mobile phones and interfaces, not everybody has a mobile phone, especially in underdeveloped countries. In those cases, alternate user interfaces such as small LCD screens, light indicators, and sounds can be used to convey results from your device.

However, if you choose to build using mobile interfaces, it is critical to recognize that developing mobile applications is not trivial. Of course, if you are a savvy programmer, you can develop an app on Android or Apple using their proprietary technologies and languages. You can build a choice of features and develop a great application. But for others who do not necessarily want a lot of features and want to develop a good and just-enough application, fortunately, there are easier options. The two most common mobile development solutions are MIT's AppInventor2 and Thunkable. The idea of these apps is to use simple drag-drop components that represent pieces of code, like Scratch programming language, to develop a complex solution like a mobile application. While AppInventor2 currently only supports Android applications, applications developed in Thunkable can be cross-platform and can be deployed in both Android and iOS. It is important to note that these tools are for simple and fast mobile application development, and users are limited to a few basic but notable features. For most scenarios, this can be enough, but if you want additional features and controls, consider learning to program specifically for Android and iOS.

Designing and Fabricating Shells and Covers

Suppose your solution needs an outer cover, waterproof case, or solid aspects—3D printing to the rescue! I know for many people, it still seems like 3D printing is foreign, but it is becoming the new thing. I have used

3D printing to create a lot of my final prototypes so that I have a clean and functional finish. The first step to any good 3D print is coming up with a great model that is easy to print, repeatable to print, and, most importantly, able to be printed. It is OKAY if it takes you a couple tries to come up with this "great model." Since you are 3D modeling your OWN design, you can tweak measurements according to what you think fits the best. Here are some basic tips on 3D modeling:

1. **Finding and Changing:** A great starting tool for new and upcoming modelers is to find basic models online and change them according to your needs. A great resource to find pre-modeled designs is "Thingiverse" or "Pinshape." If you do end up using a previously modeled design and changing it, make sure to provide credit to the original creator because they put a lot of hard work into it!

2. **Starter Modeling Tools:** As you get better at modeling, you will become ready to start building from scratch. Start with simple designs involving standard shapes such as cubes and rectangles that you know are easy to print on a 3D printer. After that, you can start experimenting with fun shapes and designs that might be a little bit more unconventional.

3. **Multiple Files:** When you have an idea and a vision in your mind, you might tend to go overboard on features and cool things you can add to it. Even though it might be a struggle to 3D print, it is always a great idea to have a couple of 3D files stored on your computer. You can have one main file with your "printable" model, and you can have one or two other files with features added to it that may not be "printable" but make your vision a reality!

 Once you have a model, I like to think that the hard part is done. It is sometimes hard to put something in your brain out into a computer, but there are some great starter software and tools that you can use to boost your confidence in modeling. I will list a few great ones in the "Resources" section.

The next step of any 3D printing process is to slice and print! This seems a lot harder than it actually is. Slicing is a method that a computer uses to be able to put your model into a form that the 3D printer understands. It cuts your model into thin disks that are added layer upon layer in your printing process. There are some great applications that will be listed under "Resources" that you can use to help with the automatic slicing of your design. However, there are some different options for the physical printing process in which slicing might already be done for you. Here are some of them listed out:

1. **Public Printers:** Like normal 2D printers, a lot of libraries have 3D printers available for you to upload your files into. Most likely, they will have a slicing software that you can use on their local computers. You can then upload your STL file (the one you download from your model) into the slicing software and start the printing process.

2. **External Sources:** Check out some of the great sites to upload 3D STL files to and then get a print, completed and polished, shipped right to your door in the matter of a couple of weeks! Some of my first prints were printed like this. It is a fairly simple process to upload your file onto the local system, and then the manufacturing company handles the slicing, printing, and shipping! A great source that I used was "Shapeways."

3. **At Home:** There are some great commercial 3D printers that you can find online. While some can be a bit pricey, try searching your local neighborhood blog or talking to people you know to see if they have a 3D printer you can borrow or use to print some basic designs. You can even see if 3D printers are available at your school, or you can try fundraising a little bit of money to get your own 3D printer. For this, you can use some of the great slicing software online to create a perfect print.

Those are some great ways to start getting involved in the world of 3D design and printing. It is not always easy on your first try, but if you stick with it, it makes it much easier to be able to go through the process. It can become like second nature!

Sensors

If your solution needs a sensor, start finding out if the sensor is available! The same goes for microcontrollers such as Arduinos or Raspberry Pis. I learned how to code both the microcontrollers myself, and you can do it yourself, too, with the immense amount of resources on the internet— plan for a longer time to build with these components.

The optimism is that all these technologies, when used the right way, free us from the mundane and allow us to focus on solving hard problems. Innovation and problem-solving are now only limited by our collective imagination.

It will be worthwhile to read articles that explore how these technologies are combined and collectively used in healthcare, education, future cities, manufacturing, food processing, and many others. This will allow you to make connections and dream about enhancing your solution with the latest innovations. Some great reading habits are annotating and staying engaged. Find little things within the book or paper you're reading that you find interesting and take note of them. By underlining, highlighting, or writing down ideas, you have more of a likeliness to stay engaged while reading.

Here is a tip! Chances are you are not planning to use much of this technology on your first go, and that is fine. This is a great reference guide for you to go back to when you are ready to use these technological advancements on your second or third alteration.

If your solution requires a background in more complex subjects such as genes, cells, and other concepts, basic courses are available to understand the concept you want to learn in different mediums. For example, you can look at doing courses about some topic that you plan to incorporate in your innovation. I completed a course about nanotechnology to get a better idea about carbon nanotubes. Some more resources on courses are linked under "Resources." You can request your teachers, parents, or anybody else to decode complex information in an easier format to gain a better skill set. You won't need to do a long-winded theory session. For example, my mom found a local nanomaterial manufacturer and passed his contact on to me. I requested that I take a tour to learn more about the chemical compositions of carbon nanotubes. I was not a chemistry expert AT ALL. My dad found a few simple videos that helped to explain ionic and covalent bonds in an easy-to-accept format. I did not even bother to memorize the whole periodic table because I did not have to! I had learned enough to keep going.

Testing It Out

Something that we commonly overlook is the testing portion of a build. Testing can be tedious, but I find it to be one of the most important parts of the innovation process. Testing validates your goals and defines the functionality of your solution. Recognizing the need for quality and baking it in your solution development process is equally important as coming up with a great idea. A solution that doesn't work consistently is a bad solution. Here is what you should start by thinking:

- What are the materials I need to test?
- Can I do it at home, or do I need to be at a lab?
- Do I need any expert help?

I must be honest and tell you that this is the part where I felt like ALL was lost. In every idea I tried to come up with and spent a lot of time on, most of the answers that I would come up with for the above would tell me that I could not successfully perform a test or build an innovation myself or did not have the capacity and ability to do so. For Tethys, my entire innovation journey came to a halt when I did not know the answers to questions such as "Where do I find carbon nanotubes?" or "How do I create them especially for me?" The answers will stare at you and say that your innovation journey is coming to a screeching stop. For example, while developing the entire solution for Epione, the core part of the variation of protein production by a gene is taking me years primarily because I did not know where to start. After reaching out to Dr. McMurray, one of my mentors, through an acquaintance in Nashville, he was kind enough to guide me in the process. We have tried it a dozen times to get the right combination of "yeast strain with OPRM1" even to do the testing.

But this is where you give yourself a break for a day, weeks, or a month and come back to the table and request some adult's guidance. Convince them of your solution as if you are marketing a product and request for all and any resources available. Do not take a "No" for the answer. If the response comes back that your idea is positively IMPOSSIBLE, put your foot down and create a story for the product you have developed and keep reaching out to mentors.

But think about alternatives and ask yourself *these* questions instead:

- What CAN I do at home? (More about creating a DIY lab in the "Resources" section.)
- Is there any simulated technology or software I can use?
- Can I partially confirm my hypothesis?
- Can I use my build and use that as a model for now?

Here is a tip! You can also look at leaving your idea as an idea and request for funding or apply for scholarships or fellowships to invest in bringing your idea to a reality and working with other organizations to develop your product further!

It is always a work in progress. But make sure to document all these ideas so you can compile them in the end and see how far you have gotten.

Coming Up Next

Congratulations on all your hard work in identifying a problem that impacts many and building a solution that tries to address it. However, it is not sufficient to stop and rest here. The solution is meaningless unless it is shared and presented to the world. In the coming chapter, the last step in the process, we will talk about taking the solution from your room to the world. Competitions are a great way to get people to notice your work and support it, and so is using the media to spread the message. We will cover all of these and more.

Name: _____

Class: _____ Date: _____

Step 4: Building Workspace

Please follow along with your teachers as you use this workspace to go through the observing process. Follow the numbers next to each activity/diagram in chronological order.

1. Basic Sketches

Draft Sketch #1

Draft Sketch #2

2. Available Materials

What materials do you have at hand?

_____

_____

_____

What materials do you think you need?

_____

_____

_____

3. Defining Features + Functionalities

Write out the top 5 features and functionalities of your prototype.

Features:

_____

_____

_____

_____

_____

Functionalities:

_____

_____

_____

_____

_____

What technology intrigues you the most, or what are you thinking about using in further prototypes of your idea?

☐ 5G Wireless

☐ Nanotechnology

☐ Power of Data Analytics

☐ Artificial Intelligence

☐ Virtual and Augmented Reality

☐ Microcontrollers and Microcomputers

☐ Wireless Communication

☐ Mobile Applications

☐ 3D Printing

☐ Sensors

☐ Genetic Engineering

☐ Other: _____

Why are you interested in this/these specific technologies?

_____

_____

_____

_____

_____

_____

_____

_____

_____

CHAPTER 7

Step 5—Communicating

Have you ever heard of stage fright? Maybe you have it; maybe it is a fear of yours? It is common everywhere amongst everyone. Before you get onstage or before you start talking to someone, your stomach becomes queasy, and suddenly you do not feel so well. That introduction leads me to my point of this chapter: Communicating.

Finally, after all of your hard work, observing, researching, and building, you are coming to the point where you have a finished product ready to share with the world. We are going to focus our time on communicating for a cause. I like to think of communicating as not something to fear but instead something to have fun doing. In this chapter, I want to take you through some of the steps to effectively share an idea or question as well as get rid of some of those lingering fears like stage fright.

So, what is communicating and sharing? Communicating allows you to show others what you have done and how you are going to continue to spread awareness about the problem or the question you are trying to solve or answer.

How do we share concepts? Like building, it is TOTALLY up to you. I find that the most effective ways to share my ideas are through speeches or presentations, usually accompanied by a slideshow. You can also share your idea by setting up a Q&A panel, a creative music composition, or anything else you think would spread your message. Before we hop on in, I want to share a personal story.

Ever since I was about five or six years old, my parents have always put me in uncomfortable situations. While that does not sound the best, it made me the person who I am today. One of my biggest fears for the longest time was speaking in public, but now that is what I do most days. Since then, I have found that the best way to get rid of your fears is to face them. When I was in second or third grade, I started doing many public speaking sessions and talking to large groups of people. I enrolled in a Toastmasters club, a club dedicated to public speaking and improving your communication skills. I was the youngest to be a part of it. Sure, I despised it at first, but now it is something that is second nature to me and something that I enjoy doing.

Presentation Skills

Based on that story, you could guess that we are talking about stage fright. Maybe it is a presentation in school or the talent show. Stage fright is normal, but it is something we can avoid. To help us overcome it, I want to go over a method I created to help us present and speak better overall:

We can use this to be aware of how we S.P.E.A.K. in public! For each one of the letters, I have a short exercise that you can do to master it!

S—Sound: Make sure you are speaking at the perfect volume—not too loud, not too soft—so that everyone in the room can hear you perfectly.

Exercise: Try recording yourself on a mobile device and listening back to it. What does your volume sound like?

P—Posture: Posture is important. Try not to fidget with your hands, and be sure to stand up straight and confident. Research shows that looking confident helps with acting confident, which helps get rid of stage fright.

Exercise: Find a mirror in your bathroom or around your house. Say this line, "My name is [Insert Name Here], and for breakfast this morning, I had..." How did you look? Did you feel confident?

E—Eye Contact: Make sure to look at who you are addressing. If you are speaking to one person, it is always good to look directly into their eyes. If it is about two or three people or any other small group, try to glance at everyone at least once by looking "through" them or at their foreheads. If it is a large crowd, keep gazing back and forth so that you keep the audience engaged.

Exercise: Look for someone who can do this exercise with you. Look them in the eyes and tell them what you had for breakfast this morning. If you look away or lose focus, try it out with another person or try it again with the same person. If you are doing well, try to add more people and see what it feels like. How did you do? Which group seemed the hardest?

A—Articulation: Articulation is important. Make sure that the words you are saying are clear for everyone to understand. This might mean going faster or slower and not fading your volume at the end of your words.

Exercise: Take this as more of a social experiment. Pick out three friends or family members you can try this with. Speak fast with one of them and tell them about what you had for breakfast, then speak slowly with another one and tell them the same thing. With the third one, use proper articulation. What were everyone's reactions? Who understood the best?

K—Knowledge: Knowing your presentation or speech helps a lot with confidence and making sure that you can spread your ideas confidently. You can try practicing or using notecards or use memorization techniques such as remembering little sections with bullet points.

Exercise: Pick out any book from your house or school, close your eyes, and flip to a random page. Try to memorize as much as you can of that page confidently and recite it to someone you know. Was it hard? What can you do to improve your memorization skills next time? Teachers, you can use this activity to "break the ice" before the first presentations.

Here is a tip! If you do get flustered and nervous, take a deep breath, and count to three slowly in your head. You know your content and speech better than anyone else. Everyone makes mistakes, and it is okay to be nervous.

I hope that helped you gain confidence while you S.P.E.A.K.! Now that we have a solid understanding of how we can improve our public speaking skills, I want to introduce a task that can help you grow your sharing capabilities and add some more creativity there.

Science Snapshot! Meet Krithik Ramesh. After understanding the complexity of spinal reconstruction, Krithik developed a live-time navigational and surgical aid utilizing computer vision systems and machine learning. Krithik communicates his message and work to students around the globe, inspiring them to pursue their scientific passions and interests.

Videos and Papers

Now that you are set to go for a great speaking opportunity or are super ready to present your ideas, it is time to understand how to build your ideas into video and paper.

Videos: Videos are the BEST way to present your information. You can even send them out to mentors, who can try them out on others and provide you feedback. Let us start with just a few main tips:

- Keep the video short.
- Catch people's attention visually.
- Be clear and concise.

These are the three main things you should focus on while creating a video. To share a concept, I like to make sure my videos are about three to four minutes long. I use animations throughout my video (great animation and video editing software can be found in the "Research" section). I also make sure that I am getting the point across as soon as possible.

Here is a tip! Videos are great to send out to experts or mentors if you are looking to get answers. The videos help to go over a topic very easily without you having to do a lot of writing! It limits the words you are sending in an email, which can help ensure you are not overwhelming the person you are reaching out to.

I can assure you the video you create will be the most precious thing for you. You can use this video for sharing in your classrooms, science exhibitions, and your local STEM clubs for getting feedback. It is your product, so nobody is as confident in its ability as you are. If you can convince yourself that your product and idea is the best, you can convince the world.

Technical Research Paper: I am learning this, and I have no qualms in saying that this is my weakest area. I just want to gather all my materials and dump them together, but a good technical paper needs formatting, concise graphs, and analysis. I have always taken the guidance of a professor to write and review this. The "Resources" page has a lot of useful information about authoring a solid research paper.

Whether it feels like it or not, you just finished the innovation process. It has been a journey, but it has been one well worth it. Your idea, and how far you have come with it, is fantastic.

A Good Audience

Before we move on to the next part, I wanted to share something that is commonly overlooked in this step, and that is a good audience. Like I said in the task, a good audience is whoever you are comfortable sharing your idea around. While this is true, you should also consider who your idea is directed to.

I had somebody from India write to me about an idea that improves energy efficiency and how to find resources since he was in a rural place. With the internet these days, I suggested he build what he can with the limited resources he has or at least draw his idea out on a piece of paper.

Another idea I suggested was to create a video of his proposal and share it with the closest local university or an organization that focuses on energy. A great tip for all of you is: Request your teachers to connect you with resources outside the school, and I am sure somebody will take the first step to help you out. I helped show him how important it was for him to communicate to get the attention he needed for further resources. I am not sure whether he is still working on it; however, the lesson is you never have to wait until you have a fully developed prototype to communicate.

Here is a tip! Try reaching out to these scholars and your target audience by responsibly using various social media platforms or even asking for help from your parents to reach out to people or hop on phone calls to pitch your ideas.

For example, with Tethys, I like to share it with water experts because they know a lot about chemical contamination in water, and I think they would love learning about it. I also like to share my product with families because my targeted audience for Tethys is households. For Epione, I like to share the idea with physicians and medical researchers because, currently, prescription opioid addiction is something that is highly researched in the medical field. For Kindly, I share it with teenagers my age and school districts to get their opinion on how I can continue to grow the idea. Finding your perfect target audience can sometimes make your ideas become a reality. When I took a focused approach to the target audience, I found people willing to invest in my idea, work alongside me, and mentor me through every step.

Coming Up Next

Now that you have officially finished the innovation process, all that is left to do is write up a research paper, find mentors, and slap a cool name on it. Right? Not yet. There is a little bit more to the innovation process than what the eyes can see. We discussed ways to communicate your ideas effectively. Next, we'll move on to learning about how to deal with failure and understanding that iteration is a natural part of the process.

Step 5: Communicating Workspace

Please follow along with your teachers as you use this workspace to go through the observing process. Follow the numbers next to each activity/ diagram in chronological order.

1. Discovering S.P.E.A.K.

Do a quick reflection on your exercises, answer the guiding questions:

How did the exercises feel?

_____

_____

What went well?

_____

_____

What do you think could have gone better?

_____

_____

What is your favorite letter in S.P.E.A.K.?

_____

_____

What are you going to improve on for next time?

_____

_____

2. Filming a 60-Second Video

Write out some bullet points about what you will include in your 60-second video:

_____

_____

_____

_____

What did you learn from filming? How will you improve your video later?

_____

_____

_____

3. Sharing your 60-Second Video

How will you share your video with the class? Circle Yes or No:

Will you have a speech to back it up?   YES   NO

Will you include a quick message about your journey?   YES   NO

Will you perform a skit or put on a play?   YES   NO

Will you create an audience experience?   YES   NO

If none apply...what will you do?

_____

_____

_____

_____

List three words to describe your entire innovation experience. It is hard, I know.

_____, _____, and _____

CHAPTER 8

Failing and Iterating

And just when you thought it was over…you realize there is another step in the process. It is not exactly a new step but a repetition of the original steps to refine your solution because it is rare that we get everything right the first time. Also called iteration. While it does seem like this will never end, iterating is not the end of the world (even though it can sometimes feel like that). Essentially, iterating is the process of making changes to your idea, whether those changes are super small or super big. When we want to solve problems, we want to end up with the best product possible so that we can get the feedback we need and so we can have an accurate representation of our effort and work. But…to do that, we need to face a few challenges.

Something we have not talked about too much is the idea of failure and where failure comes in. One of the most common reasons for iteration and making changes is a failure. Failure can come in tons of forms. For example, someone did the same thing you did (story to come later), or a piece of your idea does not seem rational. Maybe the problem that you observed, in the beginning, isn't a problem anymore, or there is a better current solution that has come out. Maybe building your solution is not as possible as you thought it was going to be!

Again, a lot of things could go wrong. But saying that, do not be discouraged. That is exactly what iteration is for: Making your ideas better than they originally were. If we think about it in detail, if we do not fail, we will never get better. Tethys originally started out as a big,

bulky device. I realized that it was too heavy, and I had to start back at the research step to see how I could reduce the size. Now it is lightweight and small enough that it is portable. If I had not identified that problem, Tethys would still be bulky and heavy to this day.

Here is a tip! Design is not the only place you can fail! Failure can occur in any phase of your innovation journey. The big idea is to go through the process without worrying about making mistakes. Many of the errors and mistakes that I made were within the testing process. Go ahead and test your solution, even if you're not sure it will work. Testing IS the time to make mistakes.

Let us introduce another fun concept: Risk. Risk is how you go after things that scare you, build up that courage knowing you might fail. Risk is my lifeline. I try to take risks in whatever I do. I tried to build that confidence within me. But you need to understand that you might often fail if you take a risk. Let us take playing the piano as an example. I have been playing the piano for about eleven years. I started when I was three years old, and the first note I ever played was middle C. I was so reluctant to join piano because it seemed hard, but I took that risk to do it. My teacher told me where middle C was and asked me to play it, and I played an F instead. I instantly decided I never want to play the piano again; it was hard, and I had already messed up. My parents urged me to go back and take that risk knowing that I would succeed if I put my mind to it. With GREAT hesitation, I said yes—under the circumstances that if I messed up again, I could quit. My parents agreed, and I practiced C for two weeks. I had a proud grin on my face and played C perfectly on the piano in my next lesson. Sure, playing that F shot me down, but playing that C perfectly boosted my confidence like nothing else. Succeeding at risk motivates and drives you to keep going, and that is how I rose from my failures. Even if I played an F while building something, I would take a break and come back later to nail that C.

I promised you a story about failure, so here goes: In fifth grade, I produced a great idea to help stop ground-based lasers from blinding pilots through windshields. It was based on metamaterials to absorb laser light frequency. I was writing a proposal for it as my "communicating step." As I was doing some last-minute research about statistics, I realized that there was an article published a day earlier about using metamaterials for airplane windshields. I was beyond devastated. I almost thought of totally giving up this idea, but I realized that "Hey! It is okay if someone did the same thing as me. I'm going to try to make it better." It took me another couple of weeks, but I came up with an idea that was even stronger than before based on Harvard research on converting any light frequency into normal light by capturing light in rubidium atoms and converting it to mass. I was so excited about this new idea and even wrote to the Harvard professor requesting feedback if I could do the same for laser lights. I ended up sharing it with my class and STEM clubs, who loved the idea, and I received an honorable mention for a breakthrough technology with a different application.

That is just one example. The important thing is to NEVER. GIVE. UP. No matter how hard it gets, persevering is the thing that can get you through anything. You must stick to it and remember that your end goal is to make a difference in society, and people need you to solve this problem for them. We can get inspiration from political and human rights activist Nelson Mandela, who said, "Do not judge me by my successes, judge me by how many times I fell down and got back up."

Now that you have your finished idea that you have shared, I want you to go back to your original observing, brainstorming, researching, and building phases and change a little something about it. Maybe you want to scrap the whole thing and start over. If that's what you want to do, DO IT! There is no harm in spending a bit more time coming up with innovative solutions. Maybe you just want to tweak something to make your idea stronger. Again, DO IT!

This right here, the object that you are holding, the sketch you are looking at, the research you have compiled, is the strongest, most finished idea that you have come up with. But it does not stop here! If you think of something else cool, keep iterating! There is never a limit to the number of times you try.

Remember what I said earlier? Name this new awesome idea. I love to name my innovations or products because it means something to me. I love Greek gods, and it is fun as a family to name the product. Take a second to realize that YOU did this...well with the help of mentors, maybe teachers, maybe many others before you who added some pieces that you used, and those who support you. You went after something that you thought was interesting, and you stuck with it through this book. Innovator's block who?

Coming Up Next

Awesome job up to here! Now we transition to the next important phase of your journey. Next, we will talk about taking your ideas to the world through competitions and being prepared and comfortable with your message, your cause, and ideas. In the next chapter, we will go deeper into the opportunities you can consider for spreading your message and sharing your story by participating in competitions, speaking in forums, and writing about it.

IMPLEMENT

"Alone we can do so little; together we can do so much."

—HELEN KELLER

This section of the book aims to show you how to have a product ready to share with your community, how to raise awareness by taking part in challenges, and a whole chapter dedicated to a foolproof way of how to present and submit your project.

CHAPTER 9

Spreading Awareness

Congratulations! Now that you have a working prototype or a partially working prototype, it is time to communicate with the users and the world beyond YOU!

The one thing that worked for me is writing out the reasons to spread awareness. It could be any of the following or all of the following, but it would be better to focus on a few goals.

- Do you want to share the problem so influential decision-makers do something about it and act? Do you want to be an activist?

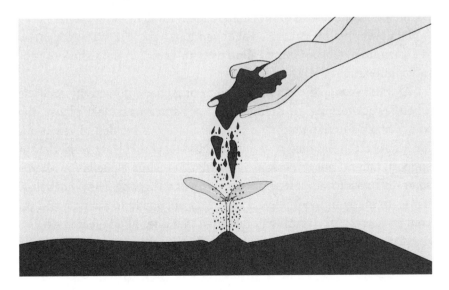

- Do you want to complete your research or product and commercialize it?
- Do you want to seek investors or collaborate with an organization for design or manufacturing?
- Do you want to reach out to universities and seek guidance from experts or professors?
- Do you want to pilot the product or pilot your idea? Pilots are great to implement a solution at a small scale where it is relatively harmless and helps us learn from it.
- Do you want to volunteer in organizations that support the awareness?
- Do you want to fundraise? Do you want to donate?

Global connection is more powerful than ever currently. It is important to decide what you want to do with your idea and how you want to impact your target audience with it. For example, the TED organization provides a global platform to share your story in the form of TED talks, TED TV, and TEDx local events. In India, a famous movie superstar Shah Rukh Khan uses the TED talk forum to invite around fifteen guests each year to share their stories of innovation, social change, and ideas in an entertaining TV show. When organizations like TED and individuals like Shah Rukh Khan make that extra effort to use their reach and social influence to support innovation and novel thought, we can only be limited in our lack of efforts to help them fulfill their mission.

Similarly, Jimmy Fallon's "Fallonventions" on NBC's Tonight Show is an example of how Jimmy Fallon uses an entertainment show to promote innovation.

Another example of the availability of global connectivity today is when I was working on Kindly, and I got stuck in certain places due to my limited understanding of AI technology. I decided to reach out for Microsoft's guidance to build my service, which they were glad to support. Later, I got to personally thank CEO Satya Nadella for Microsoft's readiness to support a stranger who was struggling. The point being, there are many individuals and organizations ready to support you on your missions if you reach out. I decided that after I had created a functional prototype of Kindly, I wanted to affect even more people. I learned about this idea of collective efficacy and soon became passionate about how we can form connections and collaboration with others using technology. Hence, I partnered with Forbes Ignite, an organization looking to bring global change in today's world, to help bring about a new idea called "Empathy Shark Tank" to help teachers and students connect with each other when they are entering a new school year or joining a new group. Even though it was not exactly using Kindly, it carried on the same message, and I encourage you to find something similar to or even a cause the same as your idea so that you can continue spreading awareness about it and letting people know that it is a problem.

But, before you share all the details of your product, to secure your intellectual property, explore whether it can be patented. You can reach out to patent lawyers or do a patent search yourself. You can start with a provisional patent and later seek further funding for a full patent once you are very sure of your next steps. For someone doing this for the first time, make sure to try and do a thorough background check as well as have some people look over your application so that you are as clear as possible.

Here is a tip! Once you understand the reasons for your communication, tailor the message for your audience, and try sharing and communicating with the tips provided in the "Communicating" chapter.

There are several ways to spread awareness. The common ones I have tried out are:

- **Blogs and Vlogs:** Seek out organizations that have the same goal. For example, I recently partnered with UNICEF to promote Kindly but, at the same time, raise awareness on internet safety. Also, try posting content on YouTube!
- **Your Events and Other Events:** Create launch events and request users to provide feedback. Try applying for scholarships to pay for and get promotional materials to help with the event.
- **Articles:** Submit articles to kids' magazine for a chance to get published. Try local newspapers or the news as well.
- **School Sessions and Workshops:** Ask your teacher if you can share your idea in class one day or as part of your grade-wide assembly.

- **Local STEM Clubs:** I reached out to the local Microsoft Store at the mall and requested that I share my idea in a DigiGirlz event to help support the participation of girls in male-dominated fields. At the same time, I conducted a session on 3D printing for the girls. STEM Scouts, a Boy Scouts of America program, has various sessions they conduct in different cities in the United States. This is a wonderful place to request an opportunity to be part of the program—to get a platform to conduct sessions for elementary students and learn more from the middle or high school STEM Scouts program.

These are just some examples, but there are MANY other creative ways to spread awareness. Let us discuss the world of social media.

Awareness through Social Media

My parents have ensured that I keep track of the time I spend on social media. It is limited and restricted to less than one hour. They have one rule for me: If I spend time there, it is not to find my self-worth on the number of likes I have, but to learn something new or spread my message. The same goes for texts and phones. Honestly, I have had times when my parents have relaxed the rule over weekends or summer, and I have noticed that social media can be a great distraction when not used properly. What I thought was just fifteen-minute browsing through the chats ended up as a waste of two hours on idle chit-chat.

There are few social-media etiquettes that I found, which I actively refer to:

- Be supportive and applaud your well-wishers.
- Do not say anything if you do not have anything nice to say.
- If you disagree, do it privately, with friends, not publicly.
- Integrity and humanity persist, not status and wealth.

There is a method that I have used to help do my part to ensure I am respectful, and I am kind to others while I use social media or texts. Let us look at how we can be CLEAR in the messages we send out.

C—Clean?

L—Lucid?

E—Edited?

A—Agreed?

R—Respectful?

I developed this method to make it as easy as possible to understand what to post online. I recommend using this to make sure that you ask yourself if your messages are C.L.E.A.R. to send out!

Clean—Make sure that you are not using any inappropriate language that could hurt someone in your messages.

Lucid—Is it easy to understand? Were you able to make sure it was expressed well and cannot be misconstrued?

Edited—Ensure that you edit your message and that it is precisely the way you want it to be and not something unintentionally hurtful. It does not hurt to rethink something.

Agreed—When possible, make sure to peer review your comment with at least one other person and get their opinion. When not possible, make sure you imagine your best friend reading your message.

Respectful—The most important one. The final check: Are your kind with your message?

This method allows me to make sure that I am being respectful of everything I am sending out! Now, the real reason I wrote this section was to discuss some of the techniques behind spreading awareness through the platform of social media. How are we able to exercise our messages in a way that reaches a big audience? Social media influencers and activists create huge impacts through the audiences they reach. Check out the "Resources" section to learn more about how you can up your social media game about spreading awareness.

CHAPTER 10

Competing with Your Idea

You might be thinking, "What does innovation have to do with competition?" It is a valid question. In fact, I started out by asking that question, and now I realize how valuable competition is to me, my process, and my idea. It builds momentum for my idea and provides harsh deadlines that force me to make it polished and better.

My biggest fear for about six to seven years was failing. Failing in any way put me down this hole that I did not want to get out of and try again. It is one of those RISKS I was talking about. There was something so scary about failing or losing that I decided the best way to avoid it was not to try and to just go with the flow. If you are like me, I GET IT. I get how hard it is to absorb failure, and I get how hard it is not to seem like the world is ending. One of the subsets of this fear was competing. I did not WANT to take that risk because, frankly, there was a high chance for failure, and I did not want to experience that.

When I was in second grade, my parents coaxed me to enter a writing contest (another risk) that I was extremely reluctant to enter. I LOVED the writing, but I did not LOVE competitions. My parents kept saying, "I think you'll like it; just try it out." After much deliberation and coaxing and hesitation...I put in some of my best work, a book report on *Ella Enchanted*. Looking back, it was not my *best* work, but it was work. To my surprise, I ended up winning second place in that challenge. If not for that one challenge, I would have never realized the importance of competing and the joy of it.

Why Compete?

Whether it is a science fair or any other challenge, competition is a terrific way to get feedback on your work and improve on it. It forces you with a deadline that helps with motivation. If you are like me, I dream of creating solutions and producing creative ways of sharing them, but as soon as some part of monotonous work starts, I procrastinate, and my project falls off the radar with other schoolwork on the plate. However, with a competition, the deadline is able to create an ending date you can't avoid and hence forced to prioritize.

No challenge is big or small when you have decided to compete. Most of us like to compete for the big cash prize and that huge recognition. Personally, I like to start with smaller competitions to share my work. Smaller competitions help me to put my thoughts together on how to communicate the solution and how you can bring awareness to the problem at hand without the pressure that a bigger competition can bring with it. Lastly, competing is a chance to check other peers' work and learn from them. This helps you improve your entry the next time.

Here is a tip! The best way to be excited about something is to start out by staying excited and not procrastinating. One of the biggest reasons to lose excitement is because you realize that there is nothing you can do in a week—but there is! Just keep up that motivation!

Now, where do you start with competitions? Here is a guide I like to follow:

- Make a list of areas that interest you and think about what format you like to present your work, such as videos, on paper, Power-Point, etc.
- Use the "Resources" section of this book or just google to find out challenges in your areas of interest. For example, last year, I wanted to know more about how roads are constructed and more about traffic management, signals, etc. A quick google search allowed me to find the ARTBA student video contest. In the process of competing, I learned so many new things by interviewing the head of transportation in my hometown. Similarly, find things you like doing at the current point in time.

- At the start of every school year or calendar year, make a list of challenges in the order of priority that you want to participate in and know their deadlines and formats of entry. Making up your mind is half the battle. Parents and teachers, you can help with this step as well! Look at the "Resources" section to check out a guide that has compiled sets of contests.
- And this one we will expand on: Determine if you want to do it alone or with a team.

Funding and Grants

A very crucial step in the innovation process is the ability to invest in materials. Materials are not cheap, and we need funding if we are serious about continuing. For example, for the prescription opioid addiction research, the materials such as antibodies specific to OPRM1 to conduct experimentation were in the range of $200-$300. Many grants can be initially received through a variety of different competitions as well as through projects, but some of the best ways to receive funding are pitching your ideas in ways that appeal to others. When I was invited to the MAKERs Women Conference, venture capitalist Ann Miura-Ko encouraged me to ask for funding by taking me back to the stage. I am glad she coaxed me to because the Female Quotient founder was generous enough to invest in my product. The investment helped me to apply for a patent, get more materials, and keep conducting my research until some partners were available to evaluate the product.

I am still uncomfortable requesting funding to support my initiatives, but there is no other option because not all of us can spend $500 per testing to conduct our research, and not all of us have access to materials that prominent labs in the country have.

If you are planning to implement a solution, look for grants that will support you. The Davidson Gifted website has a list of community service scholarships and grants that may be valuable, depending on your initiative.

Another possibility is to pitch your ideas in start-up accelerators that most cities have an organization for. I have not had any success here, but I am still trying to roll out Kindly globally.

Collaborating with Others

Collaboration or team projects can be an effective tool if you can make it work, especially when you compete and want multiple ideas to develop. Personally, I love coming up with ideas and working with a team. However, due to schedule conflicts and other commitments, I work at a pace and schedule that not all team members prefer. Hence, I keep an open mind on collaboration on my projects based on my schedule and determine whether I should join a team or proceed alone. It helps me focus once I know that I decided based on my time, and it allows me to implement MY or OUR ideas. Currently, I am working on expanding my traditional methods of working with teams. I want to develop a skill of being able to work with others effectively, to lead a team, to define action items and timelines, and lastly, to make sure we ALL play a part.

"ALL" is the biggest struggle. As someone who loves to work hard, is a perfectionist and gets things done as soon as possible, it is hard for me, like many, to work in teams or work with other people for whom innovation is not necessarily their biggest priority. If they do not measure up, I get emotionally drained following up, requesting them to contribute, and keeping the group intact. I have been training myself to learn that being an equal member of the team, it is also my responsibility to manage the team and its goals. When needed, I should be able to step up, delegate, and explicitly task what everyone needs to do, but at the same time, give the team some time to work well together.

I made a pro and con list for collaboration and produced mitigation strategies that are under my control for the cons to evaluate my options about collaboration. I want to share it with you because it really helped:

Collaboration Pros:
- Multiple perspectives for better and unique ideas
- Feedback on each element of the project or design of innovation
- Less workload when work is evenly distributed
- Teamwork, easy communication, and excitement for the next steps
- Elevated level of motivation and fun
- High accountability as each member hopes not to let down the team

Collaboration Cons:

Collaboration Needs/Pitfalls	Possible Solutions
Have to consider everyone's ideas	Creating a set Google Doc and compromising on ideas to be able to involve everyone's perspectives and everyone's talent.
Not everyone works and meets expectations	Creating a group contract or doing something fun like a team-building activity to build trust and empathy and grow expectations for each person.
Procrastination becomes the normal work habit	Creating a shared Google Drive folder or notebook to help set timelines and goals to help people stay on track. If it fails, create an emergency procedure to catch up. Also, try creating a benefits system for all the members. Ex: If we finish Goal 1 by next Tuesday, we will go to an escape room.
Other priorities which prevent team members from a meeting or working together	Adding meeting times in the calendar and Drive folder to ensure everyone is available. If not, provide meeting minutes and action items.
Everything fails, and still, other priorities prevent team members from completing their tasks	Have an open discussion, understand others' perspectives, take the lead to follow-up, and if nothing works, request team members for open peer evaluations with a third-party member. Let team members know that we will have to honestly look at who is contributing and remove others from the team to avoid failing together.

I hoped this helped you develop your perspective on if you want to work with a team or individually try. This personally opened my eyes to working with a team more often.

💡 **Here is a tip!** The future of problem-solving is a collaboration by people with different talents. Do not get me wrong! You may not need to collaborate with a student who is in your high school for a contest entry, but there is a need to collaborate with others when you innovate.

I want to introduce a new idea of picking the right team members if you do choose to work with a team. Let us take three of our friends—for example, Abby, John, and Bella. They are each a different persona.

"Hey, I'm Abby, and I don't really like working. I really like group assignments and projects because I don't have to do much of the work. I like the idea, but I just don't want to do the work. I'll wait until somebody asks me to do something. I'll pretend to work and let them know I'm busy at the last minute."	"Hey, I'm John, and I really want to help out with other projects, but I can never find the time, and I realized that it's a lot more work than I thought, so I usually decide to quit and stop helping halfway through. I do the minimum at the last minute to just contribute just because it's needed and not put in my best effort."	"Hey, I'm Bella, and I LOVE working. I usually run all my teams. However, nobody does anything as soon as I tell them, which makes me frustrated, so I end up doing it myself. I don't have the courage to let everybody know that they're not contributing, so I'll just work and add their names in the entry."

All right, so Abby, John, and Bella all have different ideas of how they participate in a team. Looking at these three, Abby does not sound like she likes working at all, John starts out excited but ends up not being motivated anymore, and Bella DOMINATES, but she does not give others a chance to pitch in and compromise on ideas.

I can tell you with no hesitation that I have been an Abby, a John, and a Bella at some point for different ideas. I realized the person I need to be if I am part of a team. Here's Bob, for an example:

"Hey, I'm Bob, and I love learning and working. Sometimes I don't feel motivated to work or be part of a team, but I tell myself that everyone is counting on me and decide to go after it. I realize that it sounds great to be a leader, and I try to be a leader, but I also don't want to dominate the conversation, so I like to take into consideration everyone's ideas. My schedules may not help me be a good team member, so I need to be upfront and not put the team at risk if I cannot contribute. I need to remove my name from the entry if I have not worked up to the expectation of others. If I commit, it's up to me to find the time. I believe I'm an effective team member for everyone."

I agree, Bob! In my perspective, this would be my ideal team member. I aim to be a Bob when I am part of a team, and I encourage you to find people like Bob for your teams and be a Bob in any team!

Last up in collaboration: I want to discuss the four steps towards collaboration, developed by psychologist Bruce Tuckman, which I keep in mind when I am working with a team. It helps me remind myself that the world does not run perfectly, and you must go with the flow to create a team that has a fantastic output:

- Forming
- Storming
- Norming
- Performing

I find this method realistic to keep in mind, especially when I am arguing with a group. Here is a first-person view for each of the steps in collaboration:

- *Forming:* It is great to meet everyone, but I am not sure how to do this.
- *Storming:* I get what we are doing, but I do not think anybody else's ideas are great.
- *Norming:* Oh! We can combine some of our ideas and identify roles.
- *Performing:* We just nailed our team project, and we worked together great at the end.

Remember, it is natural to have bumps in the collaboration process. Do not think of it as a puzzle that is already put together. Think of it as a puzzle that needs to be put together, and each of you should be playing a significant part in getting the puzzle together.

You have a great starting point here with identifying who you want to work with, but next, let us discuss ways to prepare materials for challenges and competitions.

A Competitive Advantage

First, START OUT EARLY!

It is easy to say, but it is the hardest part. If you start early, you can spend your time understanding the rules and scouting the ENTIRE website. This lets you fill out forms early, talk to people, read FAQs, browse through earlier winning submissions, and you will know about the competition. Next up, start with an idea, look for problems around you, decide what you want as your entry. My personal experience does not settle for simply entering a contest. Push your boundaries. That is when we learn. Dream big and dream the impossible. Even if you know it is impossible with your workload, go for it. Chances are it was possible, and your mind was your own constraint. Let us look at a comprehensive report, video, or other submissions. Here is what you need:

Introduction
What is the problem you are solving?
What was your inspiration (if there was one)?
Why is it a problem today (statistics are KEY here)?
What current solutions exist?
What are the gaps in these solutions?
Why the need for a new solution?
What is your idea, and how does it work?
What have you done so far?
What were the challenges you faced?
What do you want to do in the future?
Plan to commercialize
What is your business model?
Where can they find more about you or your product?
Thank you to team members, mentors, etc.
References

While lengthy, you can look at what applies most to your idea so that you have a great format ready to go for ANY entry at all. Here is a quick pitch I wrote up for Kindly using the above format:

Introduction: *(Hello, my name is Gitanjali Rao, and I love innovating and solving real-world problems using science and technology).*

Problem: *(Cyberbullying is a huge problem that affects teenagers all over the world.)*

Inspiration: *(As someone who has changed schools multiple times, cyberbullying has always been a fear of mine.)*

Statistics: *(One in five under the age of eighteen are reported for cyberbullying during the school year.)*

Current Solutions and Gaps: *(Current solutions focus on using a fixed bank of words and have the immediate goal of punishing a bully.)*

Need for Solution: *(There is a need for something more adaptive and non-punitive.)*

My Project: *(My solution, Kindly, strives to make a difference in the world of cyberbullying prevention; it uses the latest developments in artificial intelligence to help students across the world feel safer at school. It can be invoked on a variety of different platforms such as its own stand-alone app and google chrome extension. It is also non-punitive, providing bullies the chance to rethink.)*

Current Work: *(So far, I have created the front ends and have launched Kindly officially on May 2.)*

Challenges: *(It was hard to build the service itself to ensure that it learns from mistakes it made, especially since it was my first time working with machine learning.)*

Future Plans: *(In the future, I hope to implement Kindly in my school district and see it being used as another learning management system.)*

Find me at: *(Please learn more about Kindly at kindly.godaddysites. com.)*

Thank you: *(Thank you to individuals for your time, and I would be happy to answer questions.)*

Phew! You have gotten your structure down. Now start filling it out and see where and how much work you need to do, and start planning your competition entry. Ask your mentor or teacher for guidance if you are stuck. In the case of my 2019 science fair entry, I had no results because I did not get the right materials such as yeast strain with OPRM1, and I had several experimentation steps planned. My mentor and expert, Dr. McMurray, helped me to simulate the experimentation with a different yeast strain to extrapolate the conclusion while helping me to acquire materials from other labs. It is fine if you do not have all the answers!! But find an alternate way!!

Here is a tip! For an entry, no matter what medium you choose—reports, essays, videos, etc.—do what you LOVE to do in it! Be creative, like I said earlier. In one of my videos, where I wanted to share my solution for a snake-bite detection tool using thermography, I got the chance to film my ending with a snake. It was AWESOME!

The Last Stretch

Edit your work and make sure you follow all the rules. If there is a question and answer portion, make sure you are ready to go! It is YOUR work, and if you are not convinced it is yours, you cannot convince anybody else. Now, request feedback from your mentor, designated expert, or even your parents on your final work.

Here is a tip! I was always afraid to request feedback because I knew I would have more work to do. It sounds silly, but believes me, when the deadline approached, my nervousness increased. But once I crossed that thought of "more work" and saw feedback to improve my work quality and learn, it was always easier.

DON'T WAIT UNTIL THE LAST DAY! Just do it! Now, grab some ice-cream and forget about the competition...well, not completely.

You just spent so much time and effort coming up with an awesome idea and format of entry for this competition, do not waste your work! Organize and keep it in the right folders or create a website for awareness. Pick the next competition from your list and see if you can submit an enhancement of this work. If you can, start the process. You will notice that in no time, you have a full-fledged solution that is yours. Try to combine the work with your school and outside club work. Come up with a marketing plan in your marketing class or clubs such as DECA, come up with a business model if you are part of FBLA, prepare a speech in your speech and debate club about your project, etc. For those of you who do not have those clubs available, do not worry about it! You can author essays on your project in your English class with the teacher's permission, incorporate your idea in a science idea, or if you are REALLY feeling risky, you can start up a club at your own school, which focuses on building ideas!

Keep thinking of ways to improve your work in anything you do. Think of ways to bring awareness about your problem, such as writing articles, and find out ways you can help the community to solve or at least encourage others to act.

By competing, I believe our quality of work, editing skills, time management skills, and planning skills improve. You may or may not win. But if you do not enter, you will definitely not win!! You must take those risks because I know what it feels like to fail or lose a competition, and it is never pleasant when all your efforts go nowhere, But when you do take that risk, you only get better. There will be a time you will get your due recognition. It is an AMAZING and MOTIVATING feeling!

All right, let us wrap it up. It is now time for you to list the contests that you want to participate in.

Creating and Preparing Boards/Trifolds

Something you might commonly find in a competition is the need to create a poster board or a trifold or take part in an interview. As most of you know, at local science fairs, we create trifolds to educate our audience about our chosen research topic, and then we have an interactive "interview" so that they can learn even more.

I love to start creating boards with a background color scheme that is appealing to the eye, such as pale blue, gray, or green colors to emphasize the content in black font. I like to follow simple rules, like that the font size should be greater than sixteen, and titles should be bold and in a font larger than thirty-two (from sciencebuddies.com).

I usually create a layperson summary sideboard to make it easier on the judges, especially if my research consists of several hypotheses. I tend to stay away from the word "Abstract" and replace it with the word "Introduction" on the board because I was informed that I might be disqualified due to ISEF rules on not having an official abstract with a seal on the board. I do not add my name to the board because several science fairs have different rules regarding your name being on the board. I double-check to make sure I have credits or sources for pictures and other references.

A common thing that has helped me is to be ready with any trifold or other forms of boards at least a week in advance to allow time for printing, pasting, and placement on the final board. Until middle school, I used a method of printing separate pictures of my models, descriptions from PowerPoint slides and test results, and pasting them on the trifolds. While not bad, these look a bit disconnected and inconsistent with various shapes and glues that come off after a while. Last year in high school, I made it more professional by creating my entire trifold in a software publishing tool and printing the entire board at a printing center. Depending on where you are and the facilities you have available, a simple rule of thumb is to make your trifold simple and clean, focusing on rich content that supports your project or research. Less energy should be spent on assembling the content on the trifolds.

To prepare for interviews, apart from knowing your research, experimentation, and test results well, think about the following:

- What is the future of your research or project?
- What worked well, and where did you have challenges?
- Where did you fail, and what did you learn?
- What process(es) did you follow to complete your research?
- How will your research help the community, and what problem are you solving?
- What would you have done differently if you were to do it again?
- Who guided you, and how?

Time Management

The common question I get asked is, where do you get the time to innovate with so much schoolwork? It is challenging. My time management skills constantly evolve. I try to have a list of things, but with high school and academic work, it changes daily. I use my weekends and Friday after school to complete any research work. My school had an option of virtual Fridays even before the pandemic, and I took advantage of Fridays to catch up on things I wanted to do. In middle school, I traveled a lot and hence missed school. I completed my work on flights as I was raising awareness of the water quality. My biggest tip is to ask questions, for permission, details, clarifications, and more! Many schools, teachers, and principals are willing to answer your questions and make your school journey the most comfortable for you. Many schools will allow you to take breaks or receive more lenient extensions if there is a clear purpose for what you are doing and why you want to do it. When I was in fourth grade, I negotiated with my teachers to receive a fifteen-minute early dismissal from attending a STEM Scouts session because the last fifteen minutes was just choice time and packing. The more we are aware of our priorities, the easier it is to manage time and convince teachers.

I just work on one principle: commitment. If I commit to something and to somebody, then it is difficult to move away from it. I try to keep it as consistent as possible. Ninety percent of the time, I follow through on my commitments, but there is always the 10 percent where I fail because something else comes up, and my commitment is delayed, or I failed to communicate clearly. Even though I have not perfected time management, I am growing and learning more about it every day, and I am sure each one of us can improve in time management. If I commit to getting ready for my next piano lesson by letting the teacher know earlier that I will be ready with a piece in two weeks, then I focus on that and plan my time better. I tend to say no to things when I know for sure I cannot do it, or if it does not align with my goals—even if I want to be part of it. Since I have a lot of interests, I wanted to be part of several school clubs, but instead, I choose to help them when they need me. For example, my school has a Science National Honor Society that was started by another peer. I would ideally like to be part of the club since most of us are like-minded, but due to my time constraints, I just help them where I can, such as working with our school science fair coordinator to ensure the group gets the information on how to prepare for science fairs, trifold formats, deadlines, and other things—which is a one-off time commitment. It is a win-win situation where the group gets what they want, and I still get to be involved with them.

Every summer, I create a yearly plan with a priority list of what I want to focus on, and then I just stick to it as much as I can. My brother and I, on our birthdays, write a small essay on "What have we done with our time?" and "What have we done with our name?" I read a book called *Grandfather's Gold Watch* when I was six, and the protagonist of the book wrote similar essays. Recently, I've seen the value of these questions, and the process of writing answers down helps me look back at what I have done and what I can keep working on.

There are days where I go nonstop until or past midnight, and there are days where I just take a break doing nothing significant. There are days where I just procrastinate, and there are days I am just all about planning and organizing. There is no perfect solution for each one of us, and we need to find a principle we adhere to. For some of you, it may be just hard work, integrity, honesty, or selflessness. No matter what you pick, if you consistently follow that most of the time, I believe your time management skill will improve by itself because you intrinsically now know what your priority is and what you want to focus on in the time you have.

United States and Global Challenges/Camps to Participate In

Toshiba ExploraVision: The ExploraVision competition for K-12 students engages the next generation in real-world problem solving with a strong emphasis on STEM. Through this, you gain insight into building websites, creating user stories, authoring reports, creating a high-level solution, and working with a team. It is challenging! I have tried participating in this contest since I was in second grade all the way until eighth grade. I have never been a finalist, just recognized for several years with honorable mentions. However, the process of getting ready for this challenge taught me a general idea of how to look for problems and how to dream big. I always dream of the impossible in this challenge and then work backward to see what is truly feasible with the solution. The challenge taught me to look at the history of the problem that I am trying to solve or the technology that I am trying to use. That helped me understand the problems and solutions on a deeper level. As part of the challenge, we would look for the latest technologies, and I was introduced to different sensors, virtual reality, laser communication underwater, properties of light, gene editing, and more. Now, I am mentoring my brother's team to attempt this challenge! In the first year, I introduced the team to everything they needed to know about sensors. The next year, we shared AI, and even though they had a very high-level idea, they knew all the applications of it. This year we introduced them to biosensors using the piezoelectric concept.

Future Engineers: These challenges invite K-12 students to create 3D designs for space. The format has changed over the years with smaller challenges, but they are fun ones. I loved solving the simple problems and situations that were challenged to me. I created a 3D-designed tool for space and astronauts. Those were some of my first steps into the world of 3D printing. I am still not an expert in the field, but I knew enough to figure out I can create simple outer covers or design simple devices. One year, I created a simple tool for astronauts to use as a toothbrush in space, and another year, I tried a simple multi-hand tool that could collect samples from the planets they went to explore. Through this challenge, I was awarded a 3D printer, which I use to conduct elementary 3D printing workshops.

Engineer Girl Writing Contest: This was the hardest for me, but it challenged me to write. I could draw, design, and build, but I struggled writing down what I learned in a clear and concise manner. My elementary teacher, who guided me with enrichment activities for writing, was instrumental in encouraging me to try this. She understood my affinity towards science but wanted me to research and write my thoughts and solution. The first year I applied was in fourth grade, and I got great feedback from the judges even though I was not placed in the top five. It encouraged me to try it again the next year, and I was honored to receive first place. Last year, I wrote a narrative that pushed me to create a story with science, technology, and envisioning the future. The best part about this challenge is that you get the judge's feedback even if you are not in the top five, and this helps you figure out where you can improve.

4H Club Public Speaking and Demonstration: This was, by far, my favorite—but also the most nerve-racking—contest. The others that I had previously competed in were just submitting through the mail or an online portal and then I could forget about them. However, this one involved standing in front of a crowd and delivering a message. I found my need to try out a public speaking contest in elementary school when I was practicing presentations in the school. I spent time dreaming about speaking in front of huge crowds when I would see President Obama, Bill Gates, and others share their thoughts. When my mom saw my drive, she found a nearby club that provided this opportunity and a contest. I enjoyed preparing for this. All the way up to fourth grade, I loved dressing up, remembering not to fidget my thumb, and memorizing my lines. It was an experience I cherished and have the best memories of participating in. On competition day, I was participating with my friends from the 4H club, and we had a healthy competitive spirit. We would spend one Saturday morning competing for about two to three hours, after which a winner was declared to move to the county level and then state level. The prize was a certificate and ribbon, and it made us happy, and I would try again at the county and state level. About two or three years in a row, I was placed in the top three, but I learned more by observing the distinctive styles of other students. It was the positive vibes that I intrinsically absorbed. After eleven years of participating in the competition, I became confident speaking in front of a crowd.

In the demonstration contest, one year, I prepared a presentation about finances and how to invest in stock markets, bonds, or banks and about the risk/return model. This was when I was about nine years old. I learned the concept of a bull and bear market. While I did not think a lot about the importance of understanding the market at that time, the need for being financially savvy is dawning on me more as I am getting ready to graduate high school. I did not know college costs so much—in-state or out-of-state—and the additional costs of renting and food and books (as well as other expenses) are not just a few dollars. I am thankful that I chose this subject because I was taught to save, give back, and buy my necessities with the money I have. This is an important skill that our schools do not teach us. Hence I chose this topic to try demonstrating to others and leading other teens to learn from it. Once I immerse myself in a topic, the nervousness of speaking in front of a public disappears because nobody knows what I plan to say or what my knowledge of the topic is. I am the only one who has control of the content, and it is my job to engage the audience and respect their time.

Several Writing Contests—PBS Kids, Kids are Authors, Letters for Literature: Effective communication also means effective writing and the ability to convey a story. Participating in writing contests is a great way to improve writing skills. I participated in some of these contests with groups and some individually, but the thought of developing free-flowing stories without any theme or rules was fun, which is what the goals of these contests was—learning while having fun. With friends, we learned about creating cartoons. *Kids are Authors* was a story-writing contest, but participants would create graphic novels or story cartoons and submit them. It never mattered whether we won or lost when we were 7 or 8. It mattered that we had fun and learned a lot. My art skills were developed by illustrating my own books by trying these contests while they also improved my writing skill. I remember winning one year in PBS kids, and I was recognized as honorable mention a few years for Letters for Literature. Those recognitions boosted my motivation to try my best the next year. Unfortunately, I do not believe Scholastic offers the Kids are Authors contest anymore, but they have several other contests for writing that others can try.

Discovery Education 3M Young Scientist Challenge: The annual Discovery Education 3M Young Scientist Challenge invites students in grades five through eight to submit a one to a two-minute video describing a unique solution to an everyday problem for the chance to win $25,000 and an exclusive 3M mentorship. I tried this contest starting from fifth grade because a STEM and writing mentor from my local 4H club introduced me to the challenge. I did not believe that I was qualified enough because some of the projects and ideas that won were tested previously. However, that did not stop me from applying.

I used to watch the National Geographic channel a lot then, and I saw snake bites in Asia and Africa and the impacts of those bites on farmers. With little to no time for medical attention, many of them lost lives. A local professor at Belmont University gave me his Arduino and a small book associated it with and asked me to try coding. When I was learning that, I came across the concept of non-contact thermography and its ability to detect heat signatures. I just had an idea to develop a solution to quickly detect venomous snake bites in my mind due to the way the body temperature changes around the bite area, though I did not know how I would make it feasible. I put my thoughts into a PowerPoint deck and started creating a small video to communicate my solution. I had limited video editing skills. I asked my dad for software to help me with editing, and he got me a one-month subscription to We-Video. I started recording pieces and editing them myself. The first time was very tough, and if I messed up, I would restart recording. Soon, I learned to work on it efficiently.

This challenge was the first one that provided me a platform to make my idea into a reality. As part of the finalist prize package, the pairing of a mentor was life-changing for all of us. The first year I participated, I was a state winner, and the next year I was one of the top ten finalists.

eCybermission AEOP Challenge: eCYBERMISSION is a web-based science, technology, engineering, and mathematics (STEM) competition for students in grades six through nine that promotes self-discovery and enables all students to recognize the real-life applications of STEM.

I tried this because my computer science teacher at school introduced the competition to our class. The challenge is fun and engaging and is a chance to work with teams. All team members need to contribute until the end, and it helps to understand the pros and cons of working with a team. If you are selected as a regional finalist, you have a virtual chance to present your project, and if you are a finalist, you get to be in Washington DC to present it. The best thing I liked about this challenge was the ability to implement your idea with a grant.

Technovation Girls: Annually, Technovation invites teams of young people from all over the world to learn and apply the skills needed to solve real-world problems through technology. It is a girls-only challenge in which you can compete individually or in a team. I have tried this for the last three years.

I tried this individually just because I was already in between research projects. The challenge has virtual judges and provides great feedback on your coding skills and communication skills. If selected as a finalist, you will be invited to the final one-week event with a final pitch night. The best thing I liked about it was the ability to see and hear about problems from other countries and learning that what I thought was a big issue is actually a non-issue in another part of the world. It was an eye-opening experience. The challenge also helped me think about the entrepreneurship aspect of building a product and getting it into the market. I learned to research competitive products, create a SWOT analysis, build a business model, understand the dynamics of the target market, and learn the 4Ps of marketing. I was well-prepared for my high school marketing class due to participation in this contest.

TCS Discovery Education Ignite Innovation Challenge: The Ignite Innovation Student Challenge invites students in sixth through eighth grades (and at least ten years old) to share an idea for a digital solution, like a mobile app, website, robot, or wearable tech. I loved the format of this challenge because it does not bind you to develop a prototype in a short time and allows you to dream of a solution and come up with an idea which you can eventually work on. Epione was first born here. I named it differently in this challenge, but I was able to submit just an idea on what I thought would be the end-user product.

ProjectCSGirls: The challenge invites middle school girls to submit projects that are powerful in their ability to change and disrupt the present in a positive way. This is my favorite, not only because it focuses on computer science but also because of its mission to encourage middle school girls to get excited about STEM. I heard Pooja, the founder of ProjectCSGirls, speak in 2015 when she was a speaker for a Kumon National Conference. She is very kind, has a selfless personality, and she puts in a tremendous effort to encourage other girls to choose a computer science career. The thing I loved most about the final challenge is that it was a casual format which allowed me to make lifelong friends.

Genes in Space: This challenge enables students in grades seven through twelve to design DNA experiments that address a challenge in space exploration. I have now tried this three years in a row, and my guide and mentor, Ms. Kaitlyn, makes it fun for me. I have only been recognized once in eighth grade as part of a team, but the competition improved my scientific writing skills.

BizWorld Girlpreneur: This challenge invites all girls ages eight to eighteen who have a business idea or are already running a business. I have applied twice and, again, competing has helped me improve my marketing and communication skills. However, both times when I was selected as a finalist, I was unable to make it due to other commitments and had to forego my spot. However, the pictures and the final challenge details on the website were impressive, and I am sure I would have loved the experience if I had been there.

Paradigm World Challenge: The Paradigm Challenge provides an opportunity for students aged four to eighteen to use kindness, creativity, and collaboration to help address real-world problems. The challenge has certain themes, but it is still open-ended to solve problems in any way you want. This competition is my personal favorite because it explores any talent such as art, writing, music, or STEM skills. There are no rules other than to use technology to solve problems, and the focus is on "kindness." If selected as a finalist, the founder gives you a dream vacation that every child or adult, no matter the age, wants, which is a trip to Disneyland. You also receive guidance and connections to patent lawyers, who answer your questions in addition to helping you file a patent. I was impressed by the fact that the challenge does not force you to have a certain talent and that any and all forms of innovation are encouraged. The founder and his family are extremely cordial and make this a wonderful experience for you and your family.

Broadcom Masters/ISEF: Most science students know about this, and we have to take part through a local affiliated science fair. I started this just two years back to get feedback and networks to research local universities. This is a great start for somebody who wants to compete in a friendly environment where judges will interview you and give you a chance to share your research.

Kode with Klossy: I had the pleasure of meeting Karlie Kloss and sharing the stage with her at the MAKERS Conference. Her enthusiasm and energy to inspire girls around the world were infectious. I learned about the Kode With Klossy free coding camp for girls aged thirteen to eighteen that takes place across the United States. As a Kode with Klossy Scholar of 2020, I was able to gain real-world skills and solidify my coding knowledge. Not to mention I am now close to many of the girls and continue to create websites and novel solutions with them.

STEM Scouts: I was introduced to STEM Scouts in fourth grade when it was a pilot program in Tennessee. It was the first program that introduced me to visual, hands-on experiments with a detailed guide. I am still part of the STEM Scouts program, and most technologies and science concepts were introduced to me through this. Sometimes we take part in challenges through this program, and it is a fun learning environment where you learn to lead, fail, and try. You need not get the right answers, and most of the modules allow us to try, think, and try again.

There are several others that I have been part of but have not mentioned here explicitly.

The Institute of Educational Advancement provides resources on contests and challenges based on your interest area and grade. The guide is a wonderful way to start exploring and planning your calendar year on where you want to focus your energy, depending on which grade you are in. The "Resources" section provides the link for this.

I usually focus on the competitions that force me to learn a new skill and put me out of my comfort zones. Focusing on the journey to get feedback and exploring the skill sets needed to submit your entry is rewarding because these skills can be interchangeable and can be used in your high school years. In most of these experiences, the friends and networks I built are the most important outcome of competing. The one thing to remember is that you just cannot put all your energy into competing in every competition available to you, but you can plan to compete in the ones that help you grow your skills or get feedback on the innovation you are working on. You can even plan to try different competitions in different years of your elementary, middle, or high school years.

CONCLUSION

That was my story, my process, my experience, and my tips all wrapped up in one little book. There's SO MUCH MORE that I love to do and that I would love to share with you all, but there is only so much I can include.

As a recap, here is the process we used:

Old Bananas Regularly Belong in Cake

O, Step 1—Observe

B, Step 2—Brainstorm

R, Step 3—Research

B, Step 4—Build

C, Step 5—Communicate

Remember the challenge that I started at the beginning of this book? Find ONE way to change up the process that I gave you. It could be adding more time for brainstorming or another way to observe. You can even mix and switch up the steps in the order that you feel more comfortable with. It is up to you, but it only takes a second to write in the one way you want to change up the process in your innovator's notebook.

Also, take a second to look back at the first chapter. What was your end goal, and when did you start? Did you meet that goal? Did it take you a long time? Maybe it took you shorter? Innovation takes a different amount of time for everyone, and it is up to you to find the time in which you work best.

Believe it or not, this is not my process anymore. This is your process, and his/her process and everyone's process. Innovation is something that can be interpreted in a whole bunch of different ways.

Before I close this down, I want to remind you to check out my YouTube channel called "Just STEM Stuff" and blog at gitanjalijss.blog-spot.com to help you keep reading, learning, and innovating.

Here are some words of motivation. Like I always say, we are growing up in a place where we see problems that have never existed before. If you are reading this book, it means you LOVE to come up with ideas, and you want to take those first steps into innovation. I can, with no hesitation, tell you: You HAVE what it takes. Dream big, think creatively, do stuff nobody has done before, and find that drive in you. You can do anything that you want to do. Innovating is not always about getting to a conclusion or being able to share your idea as soon as possible. It is also not about doing it to compete or to win those huge cash prizes. It is about discovering ourselves and our abilities while gaining empathy, helping others, and keep going with it. One innovation can help a city, but imagine the world after thousands of innovations are launched out there. Our Earth will be in better shape than ever. Innovating is not about just getting an idea done and then retiring from it forever; it is taking that next step, finishing this episode, and moving on to the next. Problems are everywhere, and ideas can come all the time. Innovation doesn't need to stop. Take a break when needed, but I'm sure you'd want to get back to it soon. Each chapter of your work and each innovation

you make brings up more opportunities and builds more motivation in you. Make a difference, take risks, build that confidence in you. Keep innovating; keep coming up with ideas. I gave you the basic recipe, and now it is up to YOU to cook that amazing dish or bake that delicious dessert which you call your "innovation idea or product."

If you know me, I love ending with a quote from my favorite scientist, Marie Curie.

"Nothing in life is to be feared; it is only to be understood. Now is the time to understand more, so that we may fear less."

Good luck! I am counting on you.

LESSON PLANS

 ## STEP 1—Observing Lesson Plan

1. Look through the objectives of the lesson plan.
2. Choose the workspace for students to respond. Have enough copies of the book or print from the e-workspaces.
3. Ensure access to the internet for research.
4. Students can work in groups or individually.

Time: 60 minutes

Objective: Inspire students and get them excited to make a difference in this world. Enable them to observe around them and determine problems that they would like to solve.

Step 1—Inspire: Introduce young innovators to the student group to get excited.

For example, Gitanjali Rao: https://www.youtube.com/watch?v=-BN
5AyulukA

Or, other Top Young Innovators: https://time.com/collection/davos-2020/5765632/young-inventors-changing-the-world/

Step 2—Engage: Facilitate a student-led discussion on problems in the community or on students' passions. Discuss environmental problems, people problems, process problems, technology problems, and anything else they are aware of and want to solve.

Step 3—Immerse: Pick one of the problems that most of the class agrees is an important issue. Start discussing ways to fill a fishbone diagram on their workspace. The purpose of a fishbone diagram is to identify the most common causes of the main problem. Students can fill the diagram individually or in groups. They might also need some help classifying in the right category. Then, guide students towards filling out the 4-square and answering the confirmation questions. The goal of this activity is to ensure that students have found a problem they want to solve by the end of it.

Evaluation: Does each group or individual have a clear problem to tackle? Have the students gained an understanding of the problem as they completed the fishbone diagram? Have the students gained an understanding of how a problem that is sometimes too big to solve can be divided into mini-issues that can potentially be addressed? Were they able to use the 4-square methods to classify these mini problems and come up with a single problem they can solve?

 STEP 2—Brainstorming Lesson Plan

1. Look through the objectives of the lesson plan.
2. Choose the workspace for students to respond. Have enough copies of the book or print from the e-workspaces.
3. Ensure access to the internet for research.
4. Students can work in groups or individually.

Time: 60 minutes

Objective: Allow students to understand the purpose behind brainstorming and the real steps towards how to brainstorm ideas successfully.

Step 1—Inspire: Play this video for all students: https://www.ted.com/talks/luc_de_brabandere_reinventing_creative_thinking

Request students to take notes during the video or jot down words and phrases that they like or think are interesting. After the video, allow students to reflect upon the video and have them share out things that stood out to them.

Step 2—Engage: Facilitate a rapid-fire brainstorming session. Spark classroom scenarios such as: How can we make the classroom more fun? How do we make chairs more comfortable? How do we limit cheating on exams?

Step 3—Immerse: Hand out the brainstorming workspace to all the students. Start by explaining to them how to conduct initial research and guide them towards filling out their workspace. Provide students a short amount of time to brainstorm solutions to their selected problems. Remind them that the more ideas, the better. Once they have completed that, walk students through the affinity diagram and allow them to expand upon the group that they would like to focus on. The workspace also provides students a way to think ahead of their preferred research mediums.

Evaluation: Does each group or individual have a clear idea or topic that they would like to research? Do students understand the importance of "quantity" over "quality" when brainstorming ideas? Are students able to successfully fill up an affinity diagram and analyze it? Have students understood easy methods and tricks to be able to categorize a variety of solutions? Are students prepared to start the researching steps?

 STEP 3—Researching Lesson Plan

1. Look through the objectives of the lesson plan.
2. Choose the workspace for students to respond. Have enough copies of the book or print from the e-workspaces.
3. Ensure access to the internet for research.
4. Students can work in groups or individually.

Time: 60 minutes

Objective: Help students understand the fundamentals behind conducting research, communicating with others, and creating a research timeline.

Step 1—Inspire: Vote on a common topic that students are interested in. It could be a person, an object, or an activity. Provide two silent minutes and allow students to gather as much research about the chosen topic at that time.

Step 2—Engage: Have students turn to the partner next to them and discuss their opinion behind the research. Provide example discussion questions such as: Do you like researching or not? Why or why not? How do you think we can make research fun? Once the discussion is completed, provide a quick lecture about how to use matrices by creating a group matrix on the board and walking students through the process.

Step 3—Immerse: Hand out the researching workspace to all the students. On the top, allow students to think about what methods of research they prefer and put down everything they already know about their research topic of choice. Introduce the idea of mentorship and why that is important and have students draft an email to an expert/mentor. Make it clear that they might not want or need a mentor for this specific project, but drafting these emails provides practice in case they would like to reach out to a mentor. Each student or group should fill out a matrix. Keep in mind that students might need some guidance with filling it in. If students are not comfortable yet, you can always come back to matrices or fill another one out together. Lastly, students should fill out a timeline so that they can think more about where they want to take their ideas.

Evaluation: Have students created a research process that's fun and engaging for them? Are students aware of the different ways you can research and the various outputs you can receive from it? Are students confident or have a basic idea of how to use a matrix? Do students understand the importance of mentorship? Do students have a basic idea of their projected timeline?

STEP 4—Building Lesson Plan

1. Look through the objectives of the lesson plan.
2. Choose the workspace for students to respond. Have enough copies of the book or print from the e-workspaces.
3. Ensure access to the internet for research.
4. Students can work in groups or individually.

Time: 60 minutes

Objective: Help students review the basics behind how to build a solution to the problem they defined earlier and define features using technology and iterating upon builds.

Step 1—Inspire: Provide each student or group two sheets of paper and a pencil. Request each group to create a self-standing structure using only the given materials. Even though this will be challenging, students should start thinking outside the box.

Step 2—Engage: Provide a short lecture on what "building" something means and the technology that we can use behind it. Introduce concepts such as nanotechnology, genetic engineering, and artificial intelligence and allow students to take notes and draw about these various concepts. Bring up the ideas of features and functionalities and walk them through a water slide example.

Step 3—Immerse: Provide the building workspace to all students. Have students draft two of their initial sketches. Remind them that they do not need to be the most beautiful thing in the world. If they can understand it, then that is perfect! Then, guide students towards analyzing what materials they can use. Help them out by answering their questions about what is available in the classroom. Mention they can also bring in equipment from home if they would like. Guide students through the features and functionalities list and have them list the top five ideas in each. The last part allows students to demonstrate their favorite concepts that they were introduced to. This helps them identify what they would like to improve on in the future.

Evaluation: Are students confident in a variety of technology they can use to build their solutions? Can students identify what materials are available and what they need to obtain for their initial drafts? Can students define the features and functionalities of their solution? Are students adjusting to change and understanding that failure is a natural part of the process? Are students at a place where they can start to complete the first draft of their prototypes and share their work with their peers?

Communicating Lesson Plan

1. Look through the objectives of the lesson plan.
2. Choose the workspace for students to respond. Have enough copies of the book or print from the e-workspaces.
3. Ensure access to the internet for research.
4. Students can work in groups or individually.

Time: 60 minutes

Objective: Make students more comfortable with sharing their ideas and spreading awareness about the problem they are solving.

Step 1—Inspire: Let students know that you will be presenting to them today, and they will need to provide a grade. Please start by presenting your favorite animal and why that specific animal is your favorite. Have students point out things that you did well and things that you could improve on. If time permits, perform two or three scenarios, with each including something different. For example, in one scenario, you could speak quietly. In another, you could avoid eye contact, etc.

Step 2—Engage: Tell students about the S.P.E.A.K. process and start an in-class discussion. As part of the in-class discussion, participate in the exercises as labeled in the "S.P.E.A.K." section in the "Communicating" step. Students can work on exercises as a class, individually, or as a group.

Step 3—Immerse: Hand out the communicating workspace. First, allow students to reflect on their experience with the S.P.E.A.K. exercises and have them do a quick debrief on their favorite letter, what went well, and what could have gone better next time. Next, introduce to students that they will be recording a short sixty-second video to share their solution with the rest of their peers. Videos can be filmed through a phone camera, a simple camera, or, if video production is not available, a speech can be performed instead. Have students complete the planning for their sixty-second video, which should take them about fifteen to twenty minutes to draft and film. Have students present their videos or speeches. In the end, do a quick, three-word reflection for the entire innovation process. This can be done as a class or individually.

Evaluation: Are students more comfortable with S.P.E.A.K. and presenting to their peers? Have students understood more about creating videos to share their topics? Did students approach the entire innovation process with confidence and positivity? Are students able to identify their improvement points or places where they would like to continue innovating?

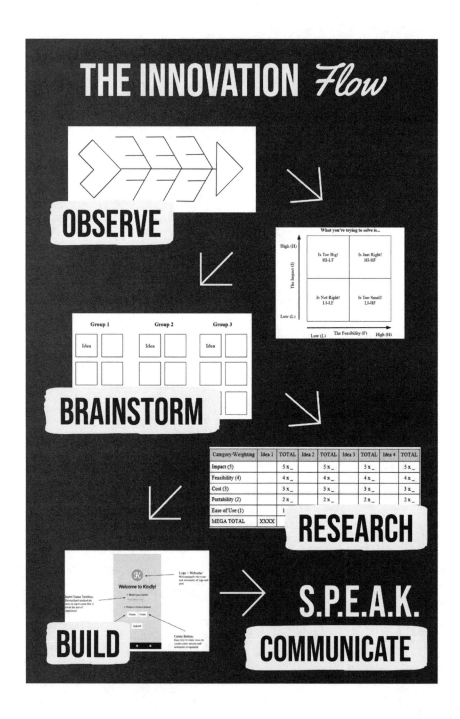

RESOURCES

Resources to maintain a growth mindset:

www.opencolleges.edu.au/informed/features/develop-a-growth
-mindset

www.mindsetworks.com/parents

blog.irisconnect.com/uk/community/blog/5-attributes-of-a-growth
-mindset-teacher

Resources for home DIY labs:

makezine.com/2017/04/11/how-to-set-up-your-own-lab

www.thoughtco.com/home-chemistry-lab-607818

blog.adafruit.com/2014/01/06/creating-a-mini-maker-space-at-home

Resources for technology, 3D design, learning how to code:

www.codecademy.com

code.org

www.technologyreview.com

www.tinkercad.com

www.khanacademy.org/computing/computer-programming

Resources for patent applications:

www.uspto.gov/patents-application-process/search-patents

www.sciencefriday.com/articles/young-inventor-file-patent

www.uspto.gov/kids/teens.html

www.sciencenewsforstudents.org/article/patent-advice-teen
-inventors

Resources for technical research papers:

www.enago.com/academy/writing-first-scientific-research-paper

www.theengineeringprojects.com/2019/06/how-to-write-a-technical-research-paper.html

www.elsevier.com/connect/how-i-published-in-a-scientific-journal
-at-age-12

Resources for creating a business model:

technovationchallenge.org/curriculum/entrepreneurship-9
-business-plan

bizkids.com/wp/wp-content/uploads/Kids-Business-Plan.pdf

homesweetroad.com/business-ideas-for-kids-business-plan

Resources for trifolds and posters:

www.societyforscience.org/broadcom-masters

www.sciencebuddies.org/science-fair-projects/competitions/
advanced-display-board-design-and-tips

www.makesigns.com

www.sciencebuddies.org/science-fair-projects/science-fair/science
-fair-project-display-boards

Resources for finding mentors:

www.nsf.gov/crssprgm/reu/list_result.jsp

www.mentoring.org/take-action/find-a-mentor

scholar.google.com

academic.microsoft.com/home

Resources for social media awareness:

influencermarketinghub.com/how-to-become-an-influencer/

blog.hootsuite.com/social-media-activism/

www.onegreenplanet.org/animalsandnature/tips-to-help-you
-become-a-better-activist-on-social-media/

Resources for grants/scholarships:

educationaladvancement.org/resource/scholarships-competitions/

educationaladvancement.org/wp-content/uploads/2018/01/
Scholarships-and-Competitions-Guide.pdf
(This is a PDF version of the above information)

www.davidsongifted.org/search-database/entry/a10483

www.davidsongifted.org/search-database/entry/a10861

scholarshipfund.org/apply/other-sources-of-tuition-assistance/

Acknowledgments

Writing this book was an arduous, but rewarding journey. However, this wouldn't have happened without the constant support and encouragement of many who were there when I was in need.

My teachers and my school, STEM School Highlands Ranch, who allowed me to imagine, explore, and to take creative risks in the classroom.

A shoutout to some of my mentors, Dr. Kathleen Shafer, Dr. Selene Hernandez-Ruiz, Ms. Jennifer Stockdale, Ms. Renee Lahti, and Dr. Michael McMurray. Thank you all for consistently believing in me.

Many organizations invested in me over the years and shared my passion for making a difference in our communities. They provided me with opportunities and resources to raise awareness on some of today's burning problems, and helped develop possible solutions through science. Most importantly, they taught me that having a vision is not enough. Developing solutions that are practical, cost effective, and scale to the challenges of the community are equally important. Thank you to all of the organizations who have worked with me through the years—especially Female Quotient, Google, Microsoft, AT&T, Jacobs, Artemide, and Hasbro, for highlighting and investing in my work.

A special thanks to the Children's Kindness Network and its founder, Mr. Ted Drier, for their work to spread awareness about kindness and involving me in their mission.

I am grateful to TED and the TEDx group of organizations, who have been instrumental in helping me share the message of kindness and innovation across the globe.

Acknowledgments

My STEM promotion partners, Mrs. Deanna Braunlin and Ms. Kaitlyn Elliott, provided valuable feedback on my process of innovation, which has made it easier for students to comprehend and adopt.

My parents, grandparents, and my younger brother were a source of constant support and patience during the long journey. I want to thank them for being with me every step of the way.

Lastly, a huge thanks to Dr. Pardis Sabeti, Dr. Cindy Moss, Ms. Tara Chklovski, and Ms. Karlie Kloss, for providing their endorsements and helping me make this book a reality.

About the Author

Gitanjali Rao was recognized as America's Top Young Scientist and received an EPA Presidential award for inventing her device "Tethys"—an early lead detection tool. Gitanjali is also the inventor of "Epione"—a device for early diagnosis of prescription opioid addiction using genetic engineering, and "Kindly"—an anti-cyberbullying service using AI and Natural Language processing.

She was honored as Forbes "30 Under 30 in Science" in 2019, TIME's "Top Young Innovator" and TIME's first "Kid of the Year" 2020 for her innovations and STEM workshops she conducts globally, which has inspired thirty-five thousand students in the last two years across four continents. In her sessions, she shares her own process of innovation that can be used by students all over the world. She is an experienced TED speaker and often presents in global and corporate forums on innovation and the importance of STEM.